LEGAL PROTECTION FOR KNOWLEDGE

LEGAL PROTECTION FOR KNOWLEDGE

Towards a New Law for Indigenous Intellectual Property

ANINDYA BHUKTA

emerald PUBLISHING

United Kingdom – North America – Japan – India
Malaysia – China

Emerald Publishing Limited
Howard House, Wagon Lane, Bingley BD16 1WA, UK

First edition 2020

British Library Cataloguing in Publication Data
A catalogue record for this book is available from the British Library

ISBN: 978-1-80043-066-2 (Print)
ISBN: 978-1-80043-063-1 (Online)
ISBN: 978-1-80043-065-5 (Epub)

INVESTOR IN PEOPLE

my wife
source of my inspiration

CONTENTS

PREFACE

Misappropriation of different types of traditional knowledge of different countries is, nowadays, a thriving business and hence a great challenge to the developing world, especially to the developing countries of the Southern hemisphere. The aboriginal communities of these developing countries, who possess this knowledge, are getting deprived as a result. The multi- national companies of developed countries, who are especially misappropriating this knowledge, neither recognize the contribution of these people, nor do they share the benefits arising out of the commercial use of this knowledge with these people. All these can happen due to the absence of any appropriate law to protect this valuable knowledge base. Presently different countries are trying to prevent these misappropriations with the help of existing intellectual property rights laws. Some *sui generis* laws have also been developed. But the problem is that most of these initiatives consider a particular dimension of this multi-dimensional knowledge suited to their objectives. What is happening as a result is that very often these laws are becoming overlapping and contradictory. To overcome this problem what is the need of the hour is to develop a comprehensive law which will encompass all the dimensions of traditional knowledge.

The objective of the present study, 'Legal Protection for Traditional Knowledge: Towards a New Law for Indigenous Intellectual Property' is to find out the lacunas of the present legislative structure and to propose the outlines of a law, its objectives and provisions that could protect the rights of the traditional knowledge holders. Accordingly, the study defines the term traditional knowledge, addresses its different dimensions and explores the economic importance of this knowledge. How this issue is addressed in different international and national forums, how different existing IPR laws try to protect the rights of knowledge-holders, what initiatives are taken by different countries – all such issues are discussed in the present treatise. The study also explains the limitations of existing laws in this regard. Finally, on the basis of the above analysis, a *sui generis* law – what should be the objectives of the law, what provisions should be included in the law – has been suggested.

The present work is the outcome of my decade-long study on different issues on intellectual property rights. It's my great pleasure that a renowned publishing house like Emerald Publishing Limited has come forward to bring my work to the notice of the world of intellectuals. I would always be indebted to all the family members of Emerald, especially to Nick Wolterman, who extended immense support to me throughout this journey with Emerald. I would also like to convey my sincere gratitude to Professor Sebak Kumar Jana of Vidyasagar University, West Bengal, for his valuable suggestions in completing the work. Above all, I must acknowledge the fact that the work would not have started at all if Professor Raj Kumar Sen had not been there to literarily insist on my serious pursuit of the project. Professor Sen is no longer among us. I shall feel his absence once more when this book finally sees the light of the day.

Anindya Bhukta
Arambagh
January 25, 2019

1

INTRODUCTION

1.1 THE PRELUDE

Voice started rising all over the world, especially in developing world, against the misappropriation and bio-piracy of traditional knowledge (TK) since the very inception of the decade 1990. As the shadow of protest got looming larger and larger, cries for the enactment of an appropriate law to protect the knowledge base of aboriginal communities in different parts of the world started pitching their volume up.

Traditional knowledge is a community-based collective knowledge. It has various dimensions, ranging from traditional cultural expressions to traditional medicines. The uniqueness of traditional knowledge lies in its transgenerational character, which flows over generations just through verbal process of transmission. The text of this knowledge is preserved nowhere in the written form. 'Traditional knowledge', as defined by World Intellectual Property Organisation (WIPO), 'generally includes the intellectual and intangible cultural heritage, practices and knowledge systems of traditional communities, including indigenous and local communities' (http://www.wipo.int/tk/en/resources/glossary.html).

Traditional knowledge is the communal knowledge of aboriginal communities. From time immemorial, these aboriginal communities have made them engaged in exploring the mother earth extensively during the search of their means of livelihood. This continuous endeavour of theirs gives us varieties of food and medicines derived from plant and animal resources. The precious knowledge of these aboriginal communities regarding nature and natural resources is, therefore, valuable to the communities themselves and also to the countries they belong to. However, neither the concerned communities nor the concerned countries ever thought of protecting this valuable intellectual property of them until before the 1930s. In fact, in the initial stages of development, it has been seen that only a few people claimed protection for their discoveries and inventions. Discoveries and inventions, at least prior to industrial revolution, were meant for the development of the entire human race of this world, scientific progress was meant for the advancement of civilization as a whole. This attitude also got reflected among the resource-rich countries, among the aboriginal communities who were exploring these resources.

Concern for protecting the rights over natural resources of the owner country and the rights of the knowledge of aboriginal communities in using these resources has never been more relevant than it has been in the twentieth and twenty-first centuries, as never before have individuals been allowed sole ownership of biological matter. The introduction of patent laws in the early1930s, which allowed plant material to be patented, has led to the current increase in both cases of and debates within the topic of biopiracy (https://sites.duke.edu/amazonbiopiracy).

Prior to 1930, patent right was granted only to non-biological matters. In order to be patentable an invention or innovation must satisfy three criteria, namely novelty, non-obviousness and applicability in industrial processes. But biological matters are essentially the gift of the nature. It is, therefore, impossible for any biological matters to satisfy the criterion of non-obviousness which refers to the presence of an inventive step. In order for an inventive step to be present, the invention or innovation must not have been obvious at the time of its creation to anyone having 'ordinary skill in the art' (Hansen & VanFleet, 2003). The protection to plant genetic resources was, naturally therefore, not sought for by anyone. Such a protection was first extended by the United States.

The United States sought for plant protection in the late 1920s. After the World War I, the US government found it difficult to put more investment in the agricultural sector through public sectors. Therefore the US government had taken a policy decision to promote and encourage the private sector in the field of agriculture (Elumalai, 2012). This policy decision led the US government to enact the Plant Patenting Act in the year 1930. The objective was to give incentive to private corporate bodies in the development of High-Yielding Varieties (HYV) seeds in their laboratories. The research towards developing HYV seeds coincidently started during this period. After World War II, many farmers in developing and industrialized countries became reliant on public breeders and private seed producers for quality seeds.

The advent of biotechnology, especially after the discovery of DNA in 1953 by Dr James Watson and Dr Francis Crick, opened up a new horizon to the breeders. As the prospect of seed business was getting brighter private corporate bodies of the US started putting pressure on their government to ensure the signing of an international treaty which would recognize the breeders' right on these newly developed seeds. The International Convention for the Protection of New Varieties of Plants (the UPOV convention) was signed by twelve developed countries in 1961 in Paris as the fall out of this corporate pressure.

Prospect of biotechnology became much brighter after the discovery of recombinant DNA technology[1] in 1973. Dr Stanley Cohen and Dr Herbert Boyer use bacterial genes to perform the first successful recombinant DNA experiment, which inserted a recombinant DNA molecule into a cell for replication.

Now all these discoveries were accentuating the probability of biopiracy. The seeds were there. The knowledge about the usage of these seeds was there. Private breeders just started collecting these seeds, modifying their characteristics a little bit with the help of modern technology and then supplying them for commercial use. Who suffered worst in this process, first of all, were the poor, underdeveloped countries, who coincidentally are the biodiversity-rich countries and, secondly, the aboriginal communities of these countries who possess the age-old knowledge of the use of these bio-resources.

As a consequence of this practice of misappropriation of biological resources and the knowledge about their uses underdeveloped countries all over the world, especially the countries of southern hemisphere, started demanding sovereign rights over their natural resources. They raised the legitimate question before the entire world: would it be possible for the breeders to breed new varieties of seeds if the mother seeds weren't supplied by them, if the basic knowledge regarding the use of these seeds weren't supplied by their aboriginal communities? If the breeders can make their seeds patented for earning, then a part of these royalties must go to the countries who own the mother seeds and also to the aboriginal communities who hold the traditional knowledge regarding the uses of these mother seeds.

A resolution to this most contentious issue came from the 22nd annual convention of Food and Agricultural Organisation of the United Nations (FAO) in 1983. In a historical Undertaking, the FAO declared plant genetic resources to be the common heritage of mankind so that it can be freely exchanged. This resolution apparently went in favour of the developed countries, because instead of recognizing sovereign rights of the states over their natural biological resources, the Undertaking established rights of every individual on any natural resources of this world. This means that anyone can freely use the biological resources of any country, which actually was the demand of the developed countries and the multi-national corporate world. But the developed countries vehemently opposed this declaration, because by this Undertaking the FAO recognized the rights of humankind not only over the natural plant materials but also over any seed newly bred in the laboratories.

The concern for protecting the rights over natural resources of the owner country and the rights of the knowledge of aboriginal communities in using these resources, therefore, in this way, were coming into prominence during the last quarter of the twenty-first century, when individual ownership were claiming over biological matters. In fact, the demand for individual ownership was more sought for after the emergence of recombinant DNA technology in 1973. This technology brought about a revolutionary change in the breeding technique. In this technology what is actually done is that a quality gene is first cut from the gene of a plant and thereafter it is inserted into the gene of another plant. A microorganism is used in this process of transformation as the carrier. The multinational corporate world, therefore, was also sought for the grant of patent, not only to biological materials but also to living organisms. Their demand was also finally granted by the

US Supreme Court in the case of *Diamond* vs. *Chakrabarty* in 1980. This historical judgment strengthened the demand for patenting biological matters.

The FAO undertaking of 1983, therefore, did not satisfy the corporate lobby. Succumbing to the mounting pressure of the lobby amendments were even made in the 1961 UPOV accord in 1991, where all the exemptions that were granted to new varieties of seeds in the 1961 treaty were revoked and the breeders were granted, in addition to the rights of production and sell of their seeds to the market, the rights of exportation and reproduction also.

However, the debate over the issue of rights of the state and the aboriginal communities did not naturally end here, because what was claimed by the resource-rich countries and their aboriginal communities was very much legitimate. To draw an end to the debate, the Biodiversity Convention of 1992 gave recognition to the state sovereignty over their biological resources. It implies that like a breeder is entitled to get royalties for his newly bred seed, the country that possesses the mother seed is also entitled to get royalties as the owner of the mother seed.

But even this effort of the Biodiversity Convention went in vain to the insistence of the developed countries and their multinational corporate. The lobby went on pressurizing in adopting the 1991 UPOV model. The fall out of this pressure is the Article 27.3(b) of the Trade Related Intellectual Property Rights (TRIPS) Agreement, which advocates for developing a *sui generis* model of law in protecting plant varieties. This law should be such as to protect the interests of all the stakeholders relating to plant materials.

Against this backdrop search for an effective law to protect the interest of the stakeholders started. The present study is only another among them.

1.2 THE PROBLEM WE ARE FACING

The advancement of civilization is the outcome of advancement of science and technology. Science and technology, however, do not always progress in the laboratories. Rather this advancement often owes havoc to the knowledge of common people. Common people gather this knowledge just by using their intellect, by the closer observation of nature and natural resources, by the hunt for food and medicines for their livelihood. More often these were team effort, rather than individual. This collective knowledge of communities is known as traditional knowledge. They are traditional in the sense that these communities have a long heritage of discovery and development of such knowledge.

Discoveries of aboriginal communities acted as an impetus to the advancement of science and technology. But they claimed nothing in return. In fact, in initial stages of human civilization discoveries in the field of science and technology progressed in this way, the discoverers never claimed any benefit in return for their discoveries. Today who does know, who discovered fire or who was the inventor of wheels? In fact, the discoverers then dedicated their discoveries for the advancement of human civilization.

However, the entire scenario started changing after the introduction of patent right in the sixteenth century. The inventors went on patenting their inventions for monetary benefits. In the twentieth century a new trend emerged. The MNCs in particular started patenting the knowledge, especially of medicinal knowledge, of aboriginal communities in their own name. This trend got accentuated after the birth of biotechnology in the 1970s.

The birth of biotechnology opened up a new horizon, especially in the field of medicines. Medicines are 'normally' derived from biological matters. Biotechnology helps genetic modification of biological matters much easier and, thereby, helps in developing much more effective drugs. The advent of biotechnology, therefore, on the one hand, has increased the importance of genetic resources and, on the other, raised the demand for TK relating to folk medicines among the MNCs. This is so because, according to figures released by the international pharmaceutical industry, it costs the industry 500–600 million dollars to introduce a new drug in the market. This is the basis for the industry's call for that stringent protection of intellectual property rights (IPR). When a company pirates a product based on TK and converts it into a medicine, it has 'acquired' a product that may be worth hundreds of millions of dollars (Sahai, 2004).

Rising demand for genetic resources along with TK eventually raised the question of protecting the interests of the holders of the traditional knowledge. But no enterprise towards extending such protection can be made full proof without legal support. Developing a legal framework for the protection of traditional knowledge is thus the need of the hour.

This need is, however, more prominent in case of countries like India. Being one of the oldest societies of the world, aboriginal communities of India, through their keen and conscious observations over the years, have built up one of the largest repositories of knowledge of medicinal preparations, method of treatment, literature, music, art forms, designs, marks etc. as well as a vast range of knowhow, skills, innovations, practices and learning. This traditional knowledge base, in a sense, has become an expression of our culture also.

The plunder of this storehouse of knowledge is, therefore, not only an invasion on our economy, but also a brutal attack on the texture of our society and culture. Moreover, since many of the indigenous communities still rely on this knowledge for their livelihood misappropriation of the knowledge can severely hamper their economic interests. Already many attempts have been made for such misappropriation. The developed countries, especially the United States, had granted several patents to some MNCs of their origin over the use of such knowledge. A popular example is the patent granted on the healing properties of turmeric. That the turmeric has healing property was the discovery of Indian traditional communities. Although India managed to revoke the patent, it does not prove that no steps should be taken any more to safeguard the interests of the traditional knowledge holders. In fact, turmeric is just one example. Many such attempts were made in the past, and in each of the case, patent were granted by the developed countries. India spent a huge amount of foreign reserve in revoking them. So, undoubtedly, it is not a standard procedure to protect traditional knowledge from being stolen away. Had India a strong legal mechanism in this regard, regular occurrence of bio-piracy wouldn't be so easy. The issue of bio-piracy was discussed at length in different international forum. The WTO categorically asked for the development of a *sui generis* law in this regard by its member countries. The development of a model law in protecting our traditional knowledge base is the objective of the present study.

1.3 RATIONALE BEHIND THE STUDY

Traditional knowledge (TK) is the information that people in a given community, based on experience and adaptation to a local culture and environment, have developed over time, and continues to develop through the process of learning and sharing by the members of the community. This kind of knowledge has never been preserved in written form. Rather they are passed over by the elderly and experts of the community orally to the generations next. When passing through generations this knowledge gained experience and became more and more refined and thereby more useful to the humankind. Not only that, journey through generations has eventually made this knowledge an integral part of the cultural identity of a community (Pant & Moorthy, 2013).

The list of TK includes knowledge, ranging from agricultural products to handicraft items, from a dancing style to mental inventories of local biological resources, animal breeds. It also includes local plant, crop and tree species; practices and technologies such as seed treatment and storage methods and tools used for planting and harvesting. In brief, the TK has several dimensions; the most noting among them are traditional knowledge relating to biological resources and traditional cultural expressions. The rationale behind protecting such knowledge can justify our search for an effective law to do the job effectively. Let us, therefore, first summarize the reasons one by one.

- TK, in most of the cases, is associated with the use of biological resources. These biological resources, in fact, not only enriches our life everyday by providing newer kind of medicines, newer varieties of goods but also it is they who are responsible for sustenance of our life in this planet by providing basic necessities of life like food, clothing and shelter made of from natural resources from time immemorial. The TK of our old people also teaches us how to keep balance in the use of natural resources so as to sustain stability in the environment. The loss of TK thus can endanger our lives and the environment as well.
- The cultural roots of a society which, in turn, creates its cultural identity as well, often lies with the local folk

culture. This local folk culture has been developed over generation by the local communities, especially aboriginal communities, of a particular area. Once this cultural traditional knowledge is allowed to be misappropriated by others there is every possibility that the cultural identity of a society be uprooted and lost forever.

- Bio-piracy of TK of a country eventually destroys the commercial advantages that the country could reap from its sale or exchange. But that's not all. By this process of misappropriation, the TK holders of the country will lose their chance of monetary benefits. These losses, of both the resource-host countries as well as the holders of TK, are impossible to be compensated.

These reasons, no doubt, justify that search for an effective law to protect the interests of the TK holders are the need of the hour. However the task is not so easy. First of all, the TK has several dimensions. Secondly, there are several stakeholders of any TK. For example, consider any TK which is associated with biological resources. Since biological resources are recognized to be national property, interest of the nation is associated with it. Again, since the knowledge base of using this resource is owned by any aboriginal community, interest of the community is also associated. Moreover, since the sustainable use of biological resources is the concern of humankind all over the world, interest of the international community is associated. Therefore, the most appropriate mechanism to protect TK is one which can simultaneously serve the interests of these different stakeholders. This is not an easy task, because the interests of different stakeholders are again often conflicting. Therefore, establishing a unique law for the protection of TK is difficult not only because the TK has different dimensions which cannot easily be addressed in a single framework of law, but also because interests of different stakeholders are different.

1.4 THE GAPS WE FOUND

A lot has been discussed on traditional knowledge. A huge number of articles have been written on misappropriation of traditional knowledge and the incompetence of existing IPR laws in preventing this misappropriation. Several attempts have been made to draw the attention to the fact that developing a singular legal framework to address the problems of TK holders is the need of the hour. But the TK has a multi-dimensional character. Owing to this character when different international institutions, organizations attempted to address the problems, it has been seen that they overlapped, reached into agreements which are contradictory. Moreover, the TK is not only multi-dimensional, but the problems of the TK holders are region specific also. As a result, the WTO in its agreement on trade-related aspects of intellectual property rights categorically mentioned the necessity of building *sui generis* laws by its member countries. But till now only a few countries have made an attempt towards this direction. Moreover, the countries who have tried so, didn't address the multi-dimensional character of the knowledge in this legal framework. Even some countries, like India, have developed more than one law to address various dimensions of the traditional knowledge, and it has been seen that they often became overlapping and contradictory. The Biodiversity Act, the Plant Varieties and Farmer's Right Act and the Seed Bill of India vividly illustrated this problem. The simple reason is that the issues they are trying to address are closely interrelated. Moreover, in trying to address different aspects of TK India overlooked some of aspects. So what is the need of the hour is to go through the problems and prospects of different dimensions of TK minutely, to identify the points of overlapping in different legal structures and on the basis of the findings try to develop a comprehensive legal framework which will encompass different dimensions of TK in a single legal framework.

1.5 OUR OBJECTIVES

In this background, the present work looks forward to (1) assess the issue of bio-piracy at length and to find out the loopholes through which the TK is being plundered away in a regular and continuous manner; (2) explore the existing laws and treaties, both at the national and international level, to examine whether they protect the interest of the holders of TK in a sufficient and suitable manner; (3) study the Access and Benefit-Sharing Mechanism of existing laws and to try to find out their lacunas; (4) find out the lacunas of the present legislative structure in order to protect the interests of the holders of the TK; and (5) suggest the structure of a model *sui generis* law that can protect the interest of the holders of the TK in a sufficient and suitable manner.

2

TRADITIONAL KNOWLEDGE: AN OVERVIEW

2.1 DEFINITION OF TRADITIONAL KNOWLEDGE

Traditional knowledge (TK) is a repertory of knowledge of a community, especially of one who is the aboriginal of a particular land, inhabits there for generations. However, it is only a snapshot view on the definitions of TK. There is no unique, universally accepted definition of TK. We, therefore, first explore various definitions of TK provided by different institutions and researchers and then try to arrive at our own.

> *TK refers to "knowledge, innovations and practices of indigenous and local communities embodying traditional lifestyles relevant for the conservation and sustainable use of biological diversity*
>
> (Article 8 (j) of the Convention on Biological Diversity)

> *TK refers to tradition-based literary, artistic or scientific works; performances; inventions; scientific discoveries; designs; marks, names and symbols;*

undisclosed information; and all other tradition-based innovations and creations resulting from intellectual activity in the industrial, scientific, literary or artistic fields. 'Tradition-based' refers to knowledge systems, creations, innovations and cultural expressions which: have generally been transmitted from generation to generation; are generally regarded as pertaining to a particular people or its territory; and, are constantly evolving in response to a changing environment. Categories of traditional knowledge could include: agricultural knowledge; scientific knowledge; technical knowledge; ecological knowledge; medicinal knowledge, including related medicines and remedies; biodiversity-related knowledge; expressions of folklore in the form of music, dance, song, handicrafts, designs, stories and artwork; elements of languages, such as names, geographical indications and symbols; and, movable cultural properties. Excluded from this description of [traditional knowledge] would be items not resulting from intellectual activity in the industrial, scientific, literary or artistic fields, such as human remains, languages in general, and other similar elements of 'heritage' in the broad sense.

(WIPO-IGC, 2002)

The indigenous people of the world possess an immense knowledge of their environments, based on centuries of living close to nature. Living in and from the richness and variety of complex ecosystems, they have an understanding of the properties of plants and animals, the functioning of ecosystems and the

> *techniques for using and managing them that is particular and often detailed. In rural communities in developing countries, locally occurring species are relied on for many – sometimes all – foods, medicines, fuel, building materials and other products. Equally, peoples' knowledge and perceptions of the environment, and their relationships with it, are often important elements of cultural identity.*
>
> (Federico Mayor, The Director General, UNESCO, 1987–1999)

> *Traditional Knowledge is a systematic way of thinking and knowing that is elaborated and applied to phenomena across biological, physical, cultural and linguistic systems. Traditional Knowledge is owned by the holders of that knowledge, often collectively, and is uniquely expressed and transmitted through indigenous languages. It is a body of knowledge generated through cultural practices, lived experiences including extensive and multigenerational observations, lessons and skills. It has been developed and verified over millennia and is still developing in a living process, including knowledge acquired today and in the future, and it is passed on from generation to generation.*
>
> (Ottawa Traditional Knowledge Principles)

2.2 DIFFERENT DIMENSIONS OF TRADITIONAL KNOWLEDGE AND THEIR USES

Traditional knowledge has several dimensions, which spreads from medicinal knowledge to cultural knowledge. In fact, it is the knowledge which people from ancient periods gathered during their struggle for existence in this world. Some such knowledge is discussed below.

2.2.1 Traditional Knowledge on Agriculture

The primary need of men is three; food, cloth and shelter. In the age of primitives, men simply collected their food from nature. They could not produce anything on their own. But with the increase in population pressure, it was becoming impossible for the mother earth to feed the entire population. Search for newer food articles started as a result. Science of agriculture became known to the human race by this process of search. Agriculture, therefore, was the primary livelihood of men on this earth. Members of aboriginal communities started exploring plants and trees in search of food. Their tireless effort ultimately opened before us a treasure house of agricultural items that can be taken by the human kind either as food or as medicine. The role of traditional knowledge can, therefore, no way be denied in respect of the development of agriculture. Today our scientific knowledge has advanced a lot. We have discovered the magic of biotechnology. Seeds are now being developed in the laboratories by the agricultural scientists. Still we are not in a position to ignore the role of our traditional farmers. Scientists can develop a new variety of seed in the laboratory, but it is only the farmers who know how to make these seeds suitable for using in different climatic conditions (Table 2.1).

2.2.2 Traditional Knowledge on Medicine

In ancient times, people used herbal medicines. Herbal medicines are medicines made of biomaterials, of plants and animals.

Table 2.1. Importance of Genetic Resources.

Sector	Size of Total Market in 2006	Importance of Genetic Resources
Pharmaceutical	US$ 640 billion	20–25% derived from genetic resources
Biotechnology	US$ 70 billion from public companies alone	Many products derived from genetic resources (enzymes, micro-organisms)
Agricultural seeds	US$ 30 billion	All derived from genetic resources
Personal care, botanical, and food and beverage industries	US$ 22 billion for herbal supplements US$ 12 billion for personal care US$ 31 billion for food products	Some products derived from genetic resources: represents 'natural' component of the market

Source: Compiled

Members of aboriginal communities, through their keen observation, discovered these medicines. Thereafter, this knowledge of them passed over generation after generation. Even today, in rural Bengal, we find some families who are known as Kabiraj family. In other provinces of India, as well as in other countries, we find such families, although in different designation. These are the families who inherit the traditional knowledge of herbal medicine.

It is, in fact, in the context of herbal medicine that the issue of biodiversity and bio-piracy has gained so much importance in today's world. Today modern medicines are mostly based on this traditional knowledge on medicine. However, the problem is that the aboriginal communities who possessed this knowledge cannot make any profit from it. This is so because the drug companies, especially, multinational companies, who actually use their knowledge do not get ready to share at least a part of their profit with these communities.

2.2.3 Traditional Cultural Expressions

A country finds its root in its cultural heritage. This heritage builds up the cultural identity of the country. However, this process of development is a long-drawn one. It develops over thousands of years. Cultural expressions, which ultimately become the part of cultural heritage of a country, therefore, are practiced for a long period of time and hence obtain the fame of 'traditional'. According to World Intellectual Protection Organization (WIPO), traditional cultural expressions are those, which (1) are handed down from one generation to another, either orally or by imitation, (2) reflect a community's cultural and social identity, (3) consist of characteristic elements of a community's heritage and (4) are made by 'authors unknown' and/or by communities and/or by individuals communally recognized as having the right, responsibility or permission to do so.

Traditional cultural expressions (TCE) may assume various forms like folk songs, rituals, paintings, oral narratives, designs, folk crafts, architectures, etc. Through these TCEs, a community's beliefs, values, wisdom, technical skills are get reflected. In fact, TCEs are the treasure house of a community's creativity and innovativeness. The importance of TCEs lies here. It is relatively easy to build up something from an already existed foundation. TCEs are the existing foundation on which something new can easily be created or invented. Possibility of piracy cannot, therefore, be anyway ruled out. Once pirated, the original holders of this knowledge would be deprived from their legitimate claim on this knowledge.

2.3 ECONOMIC IMPORTANCE OF TRADITIONAL KNOWLEDGE

The knowledge that aboriginal people acquired in the course of their search for livelihood, search for food and medicines is priceless. This valuable knowledge is known as traditional knowledge. Traditional people kept this knowledge secret and only their next generation obtained them by inheritance. To keep the secrecy of the knowledge, they were never preserved in written form, rather were passed over to the next generation orally. Despite some of this knowledge often got leaked and was misappropriated. Many of the discoverers, especially of medicine, of today's world owe their root from this misappropriated knowledge. The economic value of traditional knowledge relating to agricultural technology and medicines are therefore tremendous.

In ancient times, even some two or three centuries ago, traditional medicines were most widely used drugs. The advancement of biological sciences, chemistry and microbiology in the nineteenth and twentieth century led to the rapid development of modern medicines and thereby shifted the demand from herbal drugs to modern allopath drugs. But traditional medicines started regaining strength after the discovery of biotechnology in the twentieth century. World sales of herbal medicine were estimated at 30 billion dollars in the year 2000 which estimated to touch 5 trillion dollars by 2020. These figures exhibit the potential of herbal drugs and associated traditional knowledge. Therefore, to a country rich in biodiversity and traditional knowledge regarding the use of these resources, like India, the economic importance of traditional knowledge should be priceless. If bio-piracy and misappropriation of associated traditional knowledge can be prevented we can not only effectively reduce our health expenditure, but also be able to increase our export of medicines. Moreover, it is a fact that most of the modern medicines are being developed with the help of traditional medicinal knowledge and using plant and other bio-materials. Therefore, if developing countries can protect these resources from misappropriation they can earn a lot from the sale of these invaluable resources.

2.4 ARGUMENT FOR PROTECTING TRADITIONAL KNOWLEDGE

The modern society of today, especially of developed world, discovered the importance of the TK first during the decade of 1960 due to the emergence of biotechnology. The biotechnologist started using the TK of indigenous communities, particularly of developing and underdeveloped world of southern hemisphere, for the development of new medicines without any kind of authorization and without sharing the benefits arising out of the use of such knowledge. This act of bio-piracy is the primary reason behind developing the consciousness among the sufferer countries to protect their valuable resources. The arguments for protecting TK are as follows:

- **For medicinal benefit:** From time immemorial people all over the world used to depend on medicines derived from bio-resources for the healing of their diseases. These traditional medicines also helped them to lead a healthy and holistic life. The introduction of modern medicines began to exert a negative influence on the traditional health-care sector from the beginning of nineteenth century. The progresses made in biological sciences, microbiology, pharmacology, etc. contributed much to the fast development of modern medicines in the nineteenth and twentieth century. This, in turn, leads to a decline in the importance of traditional medicine, which, however, rebounded by the end of the twentieth century and are gaining the same day by day. Today Traditional medicine is used widely throughout the world, but especially in developing countries. In some Asian and African countries, 80% of the population depends on traditional medicine for primary health care. In many developed countries, up to 80% of the population has used some form of Complementary and Alternative Medicine (CAM), such as acupuncture. 'Traditional medicines', according to WHO,

> *...can be of different composition, including herbs, herbal materials and preparations, and finished herbal products (herbal medicines). They may also use animal materials or mineral materials. Their active ingredients are therefore substances derived from plants, animals or minerals.*
>
> (WHO, 2012)

These traditional medicines are the fruits of TK. In fact, most of the drugs all over the world today are direct or indirect derivatives of bio-resources which the indigenous healers discovered from plants and animals. This practice of indigenous healers is, therefore, to be promoted by conserving and promoting TK for a brighter prospect of humankind in this planet.

- **For advancement of science:** Recent development of genetic engineering, which is now a very fast growing branch of science, increases the importance of TK. Remember the efficacy of our age old breeders of plant and animal. They did not know the modern genetic science. Most of them did not have formal education also. Still they were able to give birth to a variety of plants and animals by the way of cross breeding. Their in-depth knowledge on plant and animal anatomy thus may be a valuable asset to our modern researchers in the branch of genetic science. Basic information about a particular thing derived from TK may save valuable time and cost in further advancement of science. If the developed nations, like today, go on trying to misappropriate this knowledge, if they don't show any interest in sharing the benefits obtained from this TK, they can never be able to reap the advantage of TK full to the brim. For reaping the advantages of this vast and in-depth knowledge of these old people we must shout their cooperation. Otherwise only a half-hearted knowledge can be acquired.

- **For conservation of environment:** Our ancestors lived in much closer proximity to nature than us. These indigenous people have an immense understanding regarding the properties of plants and animals and the techniques of using them based on their living close with nature for centuries (Bruttland, 1987).Today our farmers use pesticides and insecticides off and on to protect their crops which, in turn, ultimately become harmful not only to the field of agriculture but also to the entire environment. But farmers of yesterday were unaware of such uses. In fact pesticides and insecticides were yet to be discovered till then. So they used to use their intense knowledge about nature for the survival of their crop. They used what is called today bio pesticides and bio insecticides. The use of these bio-products not only fulfilled their objective but also kept the environment clean. Today when the environment is getting more and more polluted every day, this kind of traditional knowledge is becoming more and more relevant.

- **For ensuring food security:** Food security of a country depends mostly on the availability of variety of food crops. Developing countries, especially those in the southern hemisphere of the world, possess a rich variety of such crops. For example, in India there are 50,000 varieties of rice. This richness is the contribution of her farmers who, by their tireless effort in search of newer varieties from the mother earth, discovered a large number of varieties. Some other varieties are their own addition by the way of cross breeding and some such techniques. This knowledge of our farmers has grown over time and generations. A farmer family not only passes over this knowledge to its own predecessors but also shares it among the others farmers. This practice of sharing and saving knowledge of new seeds helped our farmers to build up a large variety of even a single crop. The variety of crops protects our food security from various natural calamities like drought and flood. This practice of sharing and saving of seeds by the indigenous farmers are now at stake. Farmers all over the world are being pressurized by the stakeholders of globalization for remaining abstain from any kind of innovation. The seeds nowadays are being produced in the laboratories of multi-national corporations. As a result in most of the cases these crops are very much fragile to natural hazards. Seeds of traditional farmers were free from such limitations, because these farmers, by their careful and devoted effort over the years made their seeds suitable for the local environment. Therefore, any effort which stands on the way of nurturing and developing traditional knowledge will be harmful in the context of food security.

- **To protect the loss of biodiversity:** Biodiversity has a great importance on our lives and livelihood. But it was the indigenous people who taught us the importance of biodiversity when their search for food and medicine discovered the same from the nature itself. The old indigenous people had great love for and close association with the nature, because it was the nature who gave them food, clothing and shelter. They came to know the importance of biodiversity by their own experience. But today, with the advancement of civilization, we are detaching ourselves from nature and thereby fail to realize the importance of biodiversity. It is thus the need of the hour to bring the TK in the public domain so that every one of us can realize how important it is to protect the biodiversity for the sake of future of human kind in this planet.

- **To safeguard the cultural identity of a nation:** As we know TK does not only mean the knowledge about plants and animals but it includes traditional cultural expressions also. TCEs, according to WIPO, refer to tangible and intangible forms in which traditional knowledge and cultures are expressed, communicated or manifested. Examples include traditional music, performances, narratives, names and symbols, designs and architectural forms (WIPO, 2012). The cultural identity of a society rests on these TCEs. Human values are also derived from these TCEs. One can easily remember the folk tales one heard from one's grandfather and grandmother. Usually all these stories contain a moral which ultimately injected moral values among us. Absence of TCEs thus certainly leads us to a valueless society.

Moreover, the cultural root of a society often lies with local folk culture. Rabindranath Tagore himself, for example, owed the lyrics of many of his songs from boul songs, which is the traditional folk song of bouls of Bengal. If we thus ignore these TCEs, our cultural heritage will certainly loss its identity.

2.5 TRADITIONAL KNOWLEDGE IN INTERNATIONAL FORA

Discussions on TK came into the forefront of international arena during the decade of 1990. In the year 1992 the Convention on Biological Diversity (CBD) was signed in the platform of United Nations Conference on Earth and Development (the Earth Summit) held at Rio de Janeiro, Brazil, which came into force in December 1993. This particular event brought international limelight for the TK.

Due to its multidimensional character TK is a complex issue to be addressed. It is, therefore, discussed in a number of fora like CBD, Food and Agriculture Organization (FAO), International Union for the Protection of New Varieties of Plants (UPOV), World Trade Organization (WTO), etc. All these institutions addressed TK from different perspectives. For example, the CBD addresses the TK on the conservation and sustainable use of various natural and bio-resources, FAO and UPOV addresses TK on genetic resources. All these approaches are necessary pre-conditions for developing sound and effective legal tools and instruments for TK protection. It is thus difficult to address and assess the TK in an appropriate manner within the context of a single institutional framework, particularly at the intergovernmental level (Vivas-Eugui, Ruiz, & Espinosa, 2003). In the present section, we shall observe how the issue of TK is addressed differently by different institutions.

2.5.1 International Milestones in Safeguarding Traditional Knowledge

1981: WIPO-UNESCO Model Law on Folklore.

1983: International Undertaking on Plant Genetic Resources adopted by the FAO.

1993: FAO international Code of Conduct for Plant

2000: Inter-Governmental Committee on Intellectual Property and Genetic Resources, Traditional Knowledge and Folklore was established by WIPO.

2001: International Treaty on Plant Genetic Resources for Food and Agriculture.

2007: UN Declaration on the Rights of Indigenous Peoples adopted.

2.5.2 The International Union for the Protection of New Varieties of Plants

Plants are essentially life forms and gift of nature. They are excluded from patentability because patent confers a kind of private property right over the patented subject matter, which should not be conferred on any product of nature. A product of nature does not also satisfy the novelty and non-obviousness criteria of patenting a product. Despite these facts the question of patenting plant varieties came into discussion in the international arena first during the second half of the twentieth century (Table 2.2).

In 1961 an international convention was held in Paris to safeguard the interest of the breeders. This convention gave birth to the International Union for the Protection of New Varieties of Plants (UPOV). The UPOV convention was originally signed by the twelve developed countries that were called the member of the Union. UPOV convention defines a basic concept of plant variety protection that must be included in the domestic laws of the members of the Union (Deeva, 2002).

The 1961 convention came into force in 1968. Thereafter, the convention went into major revisions in 1978 and 1991.

Table 2.2. A Comparison between UPOV 1978 and UPOV 1991.

UPOV Convention	1978	1991
Requirements	Distinct, uniform and stable	Distinct, uniform, stable, new
Protects	Use of reproductive material of the variety for commercial purpose	All plant varieties including plants that are derived
Duration of Protection	15 years from application date for most species. 18 years for trees and vines	20 years from application date for most species. 25 years for trees and vines
Breeder's Exemption	Yes. Acts for breeding and development of other varieties are not prohibited.	Optional. The decision to include an exemption is dependent on each member's national legislation.

UPOV, International Union for the Protection of New Varieties of Plants.

Source: http://www.bios.net/daisy/patentlens/1234.html accessed on 7.5.18

Under UPOV a breeder is defined as a person who bred, developed or discovered the variety himself or his employee to perform the aforementioned task or his successors. Such a breeder can protect his variety under this convention if the plant variety satisfies the criteria of novelty, distinctiveness, uniformity and stability.

The Novelty criteria as defined in Article 6 of 1991 Act of UPOV convention states that

The variety shall be deemed to be new if, at the date of filing of the application for a breeder's right,

> *propagating or harvested material of the variety has not been sold or otherwise disposed of to others, by or with the consent of the breeder, for purposes of exploitation of the variety: (i) in the territory of the Contracting Party in which the application has been filed earlier than one year before that date and (ii) in a territory other than that of the Contracting Party in which the application has been filed earlier than four years or, in the case of trees or of vines, earlier than six years before the said date.*

The Distinctiveness criteria as defined in Article 7 of the 1991 Act of the UPOV convention states that

> *The variety shall be deemed to be distinct if it is clearly distinguishable from any other variety whose existence is a matter of common knowledge at the time of the filing of the application. In particular, the filing of an application for the granting of a breeder's right or for the entering of another variety in an official register of varieties, in any country, shall be deemed to render that other variety a matter of common knowledge from the date of the application, provided that the application leads to the granting of a breeder's right or to the entering of the said other variety in the official register of varieties, as the case may be.*

The Uniformity criteria as defined in Article 8 of the 1991 Act of the UPOV convention states that

> *The variety shall be deemed to be uniform if, subject to the variation that may be expected from the particular features of its propagation, it is sufficiently uniform in its relevant characteristics.*

The Stability criteria as defined in Article 9 of the 1991 Act of the UPOV convention states that

> *The variety shall be deemed to be stable if its relevant characteristics remain unchanged after repeated propagation or, in the case of a particular cycle of propagation, at the end of each such cycle.*

2.5.3 Food and Agriculture Organization

The issue of protecting the TK was discussed in the FAO in relation to the definition and implementation of the concept of Farmers' Rights. But we should first know why the question of farmers' rights did arise. From the onset of the decade of 1970s, prospect of biotechnology, especially in the field of agriculture, started looming brighter. An enormous breakthrough in GMO (genetically modified organism) technology came in 1973, when Herbert Boyer and Stanley Cohen worked together to engineer the first successful genetically engineered (GE) organism. The two scientists developed a method to very specifically cut out a gene from one organism and paste it into another. Using this method, they transferred a gene that encodes antibiotic resistance from one strain of bacteria into another, bestowing antibiotic resistance upon the recipient (Rangel, 2015). The first genetically modified crop plant, an antibiotic-resistant tobacco plant, was produced in 1982. Since genetically modified crops are produced in the laboratories, mainly in the laboratories of transnational companies, by introducing genetic material of a plant into the gene of another plant, the patent right of these modified seeds is claimed by the concerned company, which, in turn, implies that even if a farmer wants to use this seed he has to purchase it every time he wants to use it. The farmer will not enjoy any right to reuse the seed. But what would happen to these researches if the mother seeds were not discovered by the farmers? In fact, it is the farmer who discovered the seeds essential for the mankind through their exploration in the jungles. But they did never claim any right over their discoveries because they worked hard only for the development of our society, not for their own material benefit. However, if today someone started claiming monetary return from the society for his invention, which invention, in turn, used the mother seed discovered once upon a time by any farmer or by a group of farmers, then, at first, the rights of these farmers should be ensured. The question of farmers' rights arose in this way. The FAO, in 1983, by its historical International Undertaking on Plant Genetic Resources (IUPGR) gave recognition to these rights of the farmers, though indirectly, by declaring in Article 1 of this Undertaking that plant genetic resources are a heritage of mankind and consequently should be available without restriction. Although this undertaking was a non-binding international agreement the developed countries, especially the multi-national companies working in the field of biotechnology vehemently opposed it because it denies rights of the breeders. The US Government also actively supported the views of their MNCs and openly lobbied for an ammendment in the IUPGR. It has successfully done in the year 1989 as an annexure 1 to the aforesaid undertaking. Annexure 1 makes it very clear that the common heritage of mankind should not affect the breeder's rights that have been enshrined in the UPOV convention (Elumalai, 2012).

The exploration, collection, conservation, maintenance and improvement of plant genetic resources are historically conducted by the farmers not by individually, but as a community. Seed technology is thus an example of TK. The recognition to this fact was given in an international treaty by FAO in the year 2001. A revision of the International

Undertaking on Plant Genetic Resources for Food and Agriculture began in 1994 which, in 2001, finally gave birth to The International Treaty on Plant Genetic Resources for Food and Agriculture. Article 9.2 of this Treaty states that:

> *The Contracting Parties agree that the responsibility for realizing Farmers' Rights, as they relate to plant genetic resources for food and agriculture, rests with national governments. In accordance with their needs and priorities, each Contracting Party should, as appropriate, and subject to its national legislation, take measures to protect and promote Farmers' Rights, including: (a) protection of traditional knowledge relevant to plant genetic resources for food and agriculture; (b) the right to equitably participate in sharing benefits arising from the utilization of plant genetic resources for food and agriculture.*
>
> (FAO, 2009)

This treaty is thus the basis for Farmer's Rights which include the protection of traditional knowledge as well as the right of benefit sharing (Deeva, 2002). However, it is narrower in scope than Article 8(j) of the CBD, and would not apply, for instance, to knowledge relating to medicinal or industrial uses of plant genetic resources (Abhilash, 2012).

2.5.4 World Intellectual Protection OrganizationWIPO

WIPO is a UN organization set up in 1967. This organization is meant to facilitate the efficient protection of intellectual property to promote the harmonization of national legislation to member states and is called upon to cooperate with relevant UN organs in promoting and facilitating the transfer of technology to developing countries in attaining their objectives in the field of science and technology and trade and development (Naresh, 2012). However, WIPO specializes particularly on protection of TK and TCE against misappropriation. In 1978 WIPO, along with the UNESCO, took its first attempt in this direction. This initiative gave birth, in 1982, to the adoption of the WIPO-UNESCO model provisions for national law on the protection of expressions of folklore against illicit exploitation and other prejudicial actions. The WIPO created a Global Intellectual Property Issues Division in 1998, which undertook several studies on TK and organized fact finding missions in different corners of the World to identify the issues at stake and the concerns of holders of the TK. Moreover, to discuss the issues of genetic resources, traditional knowledge and folklore, in the year 2000, the WIPO established an Inter-Governmental Committee on Intellectual Property and Genetic Resources, Traditional Knowledge and Folklore (IGC). The IGC was conferred the responsibility to discuss the issues concerning: (1) access to genetic resources and benefit-sharing; (2) protection of TK, whether or not associated with those resources; and (3) the protection of folklore expressions.

However, the most important initiative taken so far by the WIPO is the initiatives in signing of two international treaties, namely Patent Cooperation Treaty (PCT), 1970 and Patent Law treaty (PLT), 2000. The objective of Patent Co-operation Treaty is to allow member countries to file one Patent application which would be processed by WIPO in different WIPO member countries to avoid separate patent applications in different countries. The aim of patent law treaty, on the other hand, is to standardize the procedure for processing patent applications around the world and provide guidelines to national and regional patent offices for processing patent applications (Naresh, opcit).

2.5.5 Convention on Biological Diversity

The main objective of CBD is the conservation of biodiversity[3], sustainable use of its components along with fair and equitable sharing of benefits arising out of the utilization of biological resources[4]. The Preamble of CBD categorically states that:

> *The Contracting Partiesrecognizing the close and traditional dependence of many indigenous and local communities embodying traditional lifestyles on biological resources, and the desirability of sharing equitably benefits arising from the use of traditional knowledge, innovations and practices relevant to the conservation of biological diversity and the sustainable use of its components.*
>
> (The Preamble, Para 12, CBD, 1992)

CBD can be regarded as the first international initiative to recognize the contribution of indigenous and local communities[5] in conservation of biodiversity (Naresh, opcit). After recognizing the important role of indigenous and local communities, the Convention, in its most remarkable article (Article 8j) states that:

> *Each Contracting Party shall, as far as possible and as appropriate: Subject to its national legislation, respect, preserve and maintain knowledge, innovations and practices of indigenous and local communities embodying traditional lifestyles relevant for the conservation and sustainable use of biological*

diversity and promote their wider application with the approval and involvement of the holders of such knowledge, innovations and practices and encourage the equitable sharing of the benefits arising from the utilization of such knowledge, innovations and practices.

A close scrutiny of Article 8j, however, reveals that the Convention does not make it mandatory for the contracting parties to protect, but only to respect the rights of indigenous communities. It would be clear from the use of the phrase 'as far as possible'. But once the Convention arrives at the discussion on the TK on the use of genetic resources the language takes a U-turn. It then purposively drops this very phrase. This would be clear from the statement of Article 15:

Each Contracting Party shall, endeavour to create conditions to facilitate access to genetic resources for environmentally sound uses by other Contracting Parties and not to impose restrictions that run counter to the objectives of this Convention.

(Article 15, Para 2)

Dropping the phrase 'as far as possible' here imposes a kind of compulsion in implementing the agreement. From this change of language one may think that enough emphasis is not given to uphold the rights of the holders of the TK. But that's not true. Without Article 8j, Article 15 is meaningless. Mere access to genetic resources without the traditional knowledge associated with such genetic resources cannot yield any fruitful result and that is why in both the provisions, i.e., Article 8j and Article 15 start with the words subject to national legislation (Elumalai, opcit). The importance of the term 'national' in Article 15 can be realized only when we remember that in its Preamble the CBD recognizes States' sovereignty over their biological resources.

> *The Contracting Parties reaffirming that States have sovereign rights over their own biological resources.*
>
> (The Preamble, Para 4, CBD)

It should also be remembered in this context that it is not the CBD which first emphasises on the national sovereignty over biological resources. In fact, in the year 1962, the UN General Assembly took a resolution (No.1803) which gave recognition to States' sovereignty over their natural resources[6]. Since biological resources, as a variant of natural resources, did not gain much importance at that time, probably it was not mentioned exclusively. We got the mention of biological resources, in the name of genetic resources, in the 22nd Session of FAO–Conference in the year 1983 where genetic resources was given the status[7] of 'common heritage of mankind'. But the CBD denies this stand of FAO. Instead it

> *...relies on a well-known hypothesis in economic theory, according to which biological diversity can be protected only if it has an economic value likely to be appropriated by concerned actor. The CBD attaches therefore great importance to the property rights over biological resources as such but also over the techniques, knowledge, know-how that make their exploitation possible.*
>
> (Boisvert & Vivien, 2005)

Although, the CBD, in defining biological resources, includes genetic resources as well as other biotic components the importance is put on genetic resources. Once States sovereign rights over their own biological resources is given due recognition it automatically implies other contracting parties need to seek consent of the originating country. This is, however, explicitly mentioned in the agreement:

> *Access to genetic resources shall be subject to prior informed consent of the Contracting Party providing such resources, unless otherwise determined by that Party.*
>
> (Article 15, Para 5)

The duty of a Contracting Party, who wants to use the genetic resources of another, however, does not end here. She must come to a mutually agreed terms on the use of the genetic resources. According to the agreement:

> *Access, where granted, shall be on mutually agreed terms and subject to the provisions of this Article.*
>
> (Article 15, Para 4)

These two articles, namely PIC (Prior Informed Consent) and MAT (Mutually Agreed Terms) actually prepares a ground for the terms and conditions to be imposed regarding benefit sharing. The article regarding benefit sharing states that:

> *Each Contracting Party shall take legislative, administrative or policy measures, as appropriate, and in accordance with Articles 16 and 19 and, where necessary, through the financial mechanism established by Articles 20 and 21 with the aim of sharing in a fair and equitable way the results of research and development and the benefits arising from the commercial and other utilization of genetic resources with the Contracting Party providing such resources. Such sharing shall be upon mutually agreed terms.*
>
> (Article 15, Para 7)

Access to genetic resources, as it is already argued, is meaningless without associated technical know-how which is provided by the indigenous and local communities. These genetic resources are generally used in manufacturing industries namely drug, cosmetics etc. Manufacturing these items require intensive research in the field of biotechnology. The technical know-how of traditional communities provides important leads to this research. Keeping this point in mind the CBD in this Article 15 aims to share the benefits of research and development arising out of the use of these genetic resources. In fact, the main focus of CBD is to fully utilize the TK in ensuring conservation and sustainable use of biodiversity. The Conference of the Parties (COP) has established a working group specifically to address the implementation of Article 8 (j) and related provisions of the Convention. This Working Group is open to all Parties and indigenous and local communities' representatives play a full and active role in its work. Traditional knowledge is considered a 'cross-cutting' issue that affects many aspects of biological diversity, so it will continue to be addressed by the Conference of the Parties and by other working groups as well (CBD, 1992). Moreover, after recognizing the sovereignty of State over their biological resources and also the role of indigenous and local communities in contributing valuable clues to the modern research of biotechnology, it was imperative to take special care to uphold the provision of Article 15. Accordingly an Ad Hoc Open-ended Working Group on Access and Benefit-sharing (WGABS) was established by the Conference of Parties COP at its fifth meeting at Nairobi, Kenya in May 2000. The initial mandate of the Working Group was to develop guidelines and other approaches to assist Parties and stakeholders with the implementation of the access and benefit sharing provisions of the convention. The Working Group developed the Bonn guidelines on Access to genetic resources and fair and equitable sharing of the benefits arising out of their utilization, which were adopted by the Conference of the Parties in 2002.

2.5.6 World Trade Organization

The WTO was established in 1995 by the GATT 1994 agreement. One of the three important pillars on which the GATT is based is the set of agreements on Trade Related Aspects of Intellectual Property Rights (TRIPS). The TRIPS is an agreement that creates international rules regarding IPRs and applies to allow to members. It consolidated existing IPR laws of different countries into a single international agreement. Although TRIPS covers various IPRs such as patents, copyrights, trademarks, geographical indications, industrial designs and trade secrets, its main thrust is on patent-related issues.

In the preamble of TRIPS, intellectual property rights like patent are recognized as private rights. Under TRIPS, a patent confers exclusive rights on its owner to prevent third parties from making, using, offering for sale, selling or importing (for these purposes) the patented product; and to prevent third parties from using the patented process (and from using, selling or importing the product obtained from the patented process). IPRs owners are taken to be natural or legal persons (such as corporations and institutions). The rights are, therefore, conferred to individuals or legal entities (Naresh, opcit). Owing to this nature of TRIPS natural assets which are owned by nation states or by communities are left aside from the ambit of any protection policy. Such assets include biological resources of plant, animal and microbial origin as well as intangible assets of traditional knowledge, practices, cultural expressions, art forms and folklore belonging to rural communities (Nair, 2011).

In fact, since the introduction of first Patent Act in this world in 1790 in the United States, patenting of living organisms and/or any other bio-resources were being continuously excluded from the ambit of this Act. The simple argument was that bio-resources are the gift of nature and hence the common property of the human kind as a race. Private proprietorship cannot be imposed on it. Departing from this traditional practice it is the TRIPS who first spoke of patenting plant varieties either by patent or by an effective *sui generis* system or by any combination thereof.

Article 27.3(b) categorically stated that

> *members may exclude plants and animals other than micro-organisms, and essentially biological processes for the production of plants or animals other than non-biological and microbiological processes from patentability. However, members shall provide for the protection of plant varieties either by patents or by an effective* sui generis *system or by any combination thereof.*

The Article 27.3(b), however, also stated that the provisions of this subparagraph shall be reviewed four years after the date of entry into force of the WTO Agreement. Using this provision the demand for reviewing the Article was continuously being raised. The demand was being raised mainly because of two reasons. First of all, it is generally argued that the modern IPR regime has essentially evolved in response to a need in the aftermath of Industrial Revolution and does not in principle provide protection for the knowledge of the traditional communities in public domain (Venkataraman & Latha, 2008). Secondly, the existing IPR regime also does not provide protection for the inventions that are based on the prior existing knowledge (Cullet, 2005).

The demand for reviewing the Article 27.3(b) was being raised by the developing countries who owns a large base of traditional knowledge and who wants to protect the interest of the TK holders. The demand was finally met at the Doha Ministerial level Conference.

Discussion on TK was not explicitly mentioned in the GATT 1994 agreement. In mentioning the objectives of TRIPS (Article 7), it was only stated that the protection and enforcement of intellectual property rights should contribute to the promotion of technological innovation and to the transfer and dissemination of technology, to the mutual advantage of producers and users of technological knowledge. The developing countries started raising the issue of protecting the TK because they knew that their strength of knowledge lies in their community knowledge regarding nature and natural resources, especially of biological resources. Since the Article 27.3(b) speaks of protecting plants, animals and associated biological resources, the developing countries raised the demand for reviewing the same. The review of Article 27.3(b) began in 1999. The TRIPS Council's discussions included the following:

- How to deal with the commercial use of traditional knowledge and genetic material by those other than the communities or countries where these originate, especially when these are the subject of patent applications

- How to ensure that the TRIPS Agreement and the UN Convention on Biological Diversity (CBD) support each other.

A decision finaly came at Doha. The Doha Declaration, in Paragraph 19, has mandated the Council for TRIPS to examine the relationship between the TRIPS Agreement and the Convention on Biological Diversity, the protection of traditional knowledge and folklore, and other relevant new developments raised by the member countries. The Ministerial Declaration has instructed the Council for TRIPS to consider the demand for the protection of TK in its various work programmes including the review of Article 27.3(b) of the TRIPS. It is an important step in the post-TRIPS regime as far as the issue of protection of TK is concerned (Lukose, 2009).

3

BIO-PIRACY

3.1 DEFINITION OF BIO-PIRACY

Bio-piracy is not uniquely defined. But it simply means unauthorised use of bio-resources of a country either by the individuals or institutions or companies of other countries.

According to WTO glossary, piracy means 'unauthorised copying of materials protected by intellectual property rights (such as patents, copyright, trademarks, geographical indications, etc) for commercial dealing in copied materials'. The WTO never used the term bio-piracy. The reason lies in the fact that although the WTO is defined to be a forum for both developed and underdeveloped countries, it practically looks for the interest of the developed countries. To realize this argument against the WTO we have to understand first how the multi-national companies (MNCs) of the developed countries are snatching away the bio-resources and also the knowledge of their uses from developing countries and tried to establish their proprietorship over these stolen resources.

By natural distribution of global resources, the under-developed countries of the World have become the storehouse of bio-resources. The indigenous communities of these countries, through their keen observation on nature and natural resources and intense search for food and medicine discovered the use of these natural gifts. But after the invention of biotechnology in the 1970s, the MNCs of the developed countries certainly discovered immense profit prospect from the use of this knowledge of indigenous communities. The plundering of this traditional knowledge along with the bio-resources of the underdeveloped countries started with immediate effect. These MNCs, thereafter, started patenting the products they developed by using this knowledge and bio-resources in their own name.

It is against this malpractice of developed countries a Canadian activist Pat Mooney first coined the term bio-piracy (Mgbeoji, 2001). After obtaining the patent right the MNCs started accusing underdeveloped countries of pirating or unlawfully appropriating for their intellectual property rights. It is at this juncture the Third World countries started counteracting First World countries for misappropriating the knowledge of their indigenous people. This allegation of misappropriation was then termed bio-piracy. Bio-piracy is thus meant for unauthorized appropriation of bio-resources and associated knowledge regarding their uses without making proper compensation to the indigenous people who originally possess this knowledge, and to the countries as well who owns the biological resources.

3.2 ECONOMIC IMPACTS OF BIO-PIRACY

Food and medicines are two most important elements essential for human survival. Fortunately enough, both of these ingredients are supplied freely by the mother earth. Biological materials of plants and animals are the main sources of food and medicines. Therefore, countries of Southern hemisphere, which are rich in bio-resources, are considered as the most fortunate land of this planet. The South is the source of 90% of the world's biological wealth. India, for example, has 81,000 species of fauna and 47,000 of flora, including 15,000 plant varieties unique to the country. Yet industrial countries hold 97% of all patents worldwide and are driving the rush to patent plant genetic resources (Baxter, Mayer, & Wijeratna, 1999).

But the dark side of this fortune is that in most of the cases the biodiversity rich countries, majority of whom are developing, lack technical knowledge of using these resources in industrial processes. The developed countries, rich in technology but poor in resources, are taking the advantage of this slackness of the developing world. They are continuously using these bio-resources for their own. In return, developing countries have been paid only an infinitesimal fraction of the value for the raw materials and knowledge they contribute (ETC Group, 2002). Nevertheless the United Nations Development Program (UNDP) claimed in 2001 that a 2% royalty charge levied by developing countries on genetic materials developed by local communities in the southern hemisphere that have been patented in the industrialized North would generate more than $5 billion from medicinal plants alone (UNDP, 2001). Therefore, it isn't difficult to understand the detrimental effects of this bio-piracy on the socio-economic life of people of poor, but resource-rich, countries. Some such effects are as follows:

- **Effect on the livelihood of indigenous people:** Bio-piracy affects the lives of indigenous communities of less developed countries who depend entirely on bio-resources for their livelihood. These communities include mainly farmers and traditional healers. In fact, the farmers of these countries supply, not only to the people of their own land but also to the people of the entire world, varieties of food articles through their tireless endeavor in search of new varieties of vegetation. Sometimes they found new food plants only through their exploration over the mother earth and sometimes by using traditional cross breeding technique. Many plant varieties have originated in the seeds that farmers have selected and sown for thousands of years. Such practices of on-farm experimentation and conservation 'form the basis of food security and livelihoods for communities throughout the developing world' (UNDP, 2003). The traditional healers have also done the same job for the humankind. They engaged themselves in search of medicinal properties of plants and animals. This process of search, on the one hand, provides them their livelihood and, on the other, gives the entire human race food and medicines. Bio-piracy, therefore, is making the livelihood of indigenous people extremely difficult and endangered.

- **Effect on food security**: Bio-piracy, nowadays, is posing a threat to the food security of the victim countries. Seeds were being taken away by the multi-nationals (MNCs) unauthorized. By taking away mother seeds, the MNCs are developing new varieties of seeds from the mother seed, and then they are claiming patent right over these new varieties, which are generally high-yielding and thereby cheap in comparison to the return they promise. These cheap, high-yielding seeds are eventually kicking off the original seed from competition. The countries with enormous varieties of original seeds are thus losing their food varieties and, in ultimate course, moving towards food insecurity in their own land (Bhattacharya, 2014).
- **Effect on health security**: A large number of people, around 80% of the population, in developing countries rely largely on plant-based drugs for their health care needs. One of the reasons behind this practice is the low cost of these

traditional medicines. Traditional medicines are less costly because they are not patented drugs. Local traditional healers make these medicines from locally available bio-resources. They neither have to purchase the ingredients from the market, nor have to pay to the marketing intermediaries in order to market their products. But once these medicines are patented by the MNCs, they will be available only at medicine shops at high prices, unaffordable to the poor people of the underdeveloped countries.

- **Effect on exchequer:** Bio-piracy, on the one hand, negatively affects the export potential of the country and, on the other, increases the import burden on the exchequer. Countries rich in traditional knowledge, like India, are net exporter of herbal medicines. Once the MNCs of the developed countries are able to acquire the patent right over such medicines, they will prevent the original inventors to sell their product in the world market. Conversely they have to import the same drug from the developed countries. Burden on exchequer increases another way due to bio-piracy. The giant MNCs in the seed sector are modifying the new seeds genetically in such a way that a seed, once used, cannot be saved for further use. This means that the farmers' have to purchase seeds every year from these MNCs and to give up their traditional practice of saving and exchanging seeds with their fellow farmers. This will increase not only the cost of cultivation of the farmers, but also the burden on the foreign exchange reserve of the country.
- **Effect on biodiversity:** Different species of flora and fauna, used as ingredients to traditional medicines, are becoming either extinct or endangered due to rapid plundering. It has a detrimental effect on environment, which, in turn, affects the economy.

Among these effects, two most important are discussed in detail in the following sub-sections.

3.2.1 A Threat to Food Security

Food security in different parts of the world is now endangered. One of the reasons behind such a situation is the unabated piracy of bio-resources and associated traditional knowledge. Giant MNCs of the world, backed by the present IPR system, especially which was introduced by the Trade Related Intellectual Property Rights (TRIPS) agreement of WTO, are now challenging the food security of different countries. Vandana Shiva, in an article, writes that, by making seed-saving and seed-sharing criminal acts

> *The Agreement on Agriculture legalises the dumping of genetically engineered foods on countries and criminalises actions to protect the biological and cultural diversity on which diverse food systems are based.*
>
> (Shiva, 1993).

'Food security', as defined by 1996 World Food Summit (WFS) 'exists when all people, at all times, have physical, social and economic access to sufficient, safe and nutritious food which meets their dietary needs and food preferences for an active and healthy life'. Food insecurity, on the other hand, refers to the non-availability of food. The Food and Agriculture Organization (FAO) defines food insecurity as: 'A situation that exists when people lack secure access to sufficient amounts of safe and nutritious food for normal growth and development and an active and healthy life.' Any analysis of food security will examine whether a change from security to insecurity or insecurity to security actually takes place and also the probability of such a change happening. Factors that may lead to a situation of food insecurity include non-availability of food, lack of access, improper utilization and instability over a certain time period (Muro & Mazziotta, 2010).

During or after 1960s, green revolution took place in different countries of the world, including India. Thereafter, excessive dependency on high-yielding varieties (HYV) seeds and accompanying inputs has resulted in the slow disappearance of traditional crop varieties. For example,

> *...in the Indian state of Andhra Pradesh, one study found that the incursion of the Green Revolution led to a loss of 95% of traditional rice varieties without their collection or documentation.*
>
> (Grain, 2001).

The green revolution introduced a mono-cropping culture. Mono-cropping means planting one variety of a plant. The most obvious danger of mono-cropping is that the practice can be catastrophic if the crop is afflicted by disease (Brown, 2002). The chance of being affected by diseases is also very high in case of HYV seeds. The new rice varieties introduced by the Philippines-based International Rice Research Institute (IRRI) in the late 1960s proved vulnerable to pests and diseases. In the Indian state of Punjab, insects and pests which, prior to the Green Revolution had proven to be insignificant, became major problems with the onset of new rice varieties. By 1991, rice cultivation in the Punjab had become vulnerable to 'about 40 insects and 12 diseases' (Shiva, 1993).

Before the introduction of HYV seeds, new varieties of seeds were either discovered or bred by the traditional farmers. The farmers, all over the world, from time immemorial, made them engaged in search of plants with nutritional and medicinal values from a vast pool of wild plant varieties. In this process they discovered varieties of edible and medicinal plant resource. Their endeavour, however, did not end here. They, thereafter, tried to breed new plant varieties from the varieties available to them by cross-breeding, the process which they learnt from the natural pollinators. The plant varieties either discovered or bred in this way proved to be tolerant to local climatic conditions and hence were little prone to diseases, except the attack of new bacteria.

However, this is not the case for HYV seeds or recently introduced genetically modified (GM) crops, because they are never tested OK to be suitable for cultivation in different climatic conditions. As a result, these seeds are prone to diseases. Green Revolution, in this way, by introducing mono-cropping culture, not only increases the cost of cultivation but also pushed a large number of farmers to a high-risk zone. Cost of cultivation increase because along with seeds the farmers have to purchase chemical fertilizers, pesticides and insecticides to get a good harvest. But even then, sometimes, they are facing situations of crop failure due to the attack of unknown bacteria.

The distress of farmers has increased a lot after the emergence of GM seeds. First of all, GM seeds raise the cost of cultivation by monopolizing the seed business in the hands of a few. These big seed multi-nationals were originally engaged in the business of pesticides and insecticides. Advancement in biotechnology in the 1980s opened up new opportunities of business to them. Using biotechnology when scientists became able to insert insecticide-resistant genes to the seeds, these companies discovered a new profit prospect to be added to their existing business. The laboratories of these insecticide companies started giving birth to seeds which are resistant to various insects except the particular insect against which the company is producing its own. What happened as a result was that the farmers who were purchasing the seed of a particular company were also compelled to purchase the insecticide of the same company. The consolidation of seed and insecticide business in this way gave birth to five so called 'Gene Giants', namely DuPont, Pharmacia, Syngenta, Dow and Aventis – laying claim to a global market share of 60% of the pesticide industry, 25% of the world's seed market and almost 100% of GM crops (Meek, 2000). In ultimate course, the monopoly control over the seed business by these firms leads to increasing cost of cultivation. Moreover, to tighten their grip over the market, these companies often form illegal cartel. A consortium of farmers in the United States and other countries once alleged that from 1996 onwards corporations like Monsanto, DuPont, Dow Chemical, Novartis, AstraZeneca and some other entered into a licensing arrangement to create a cartel in which Monsanto would be the 'hub' of the GM industry, and the co-conspirators the 'spokes' (Downes, 2003).

Secondly, taking monopoly control over the market by the MNCs became easier because technology allowed them to develop seeds which can be used once-for-all. The farmers, therefore, have to give up their traditional practice of saving and sharing of seeds. In addition to this technological help, the MNCs are also taking the help of law in order to prevent this age-old culture altogether. For example, the proposed Seed Bill of our country prohibited saving and sharing of seeds by the farmers.

Thirdly, herbicide-resistant plants kill weeds which are an essential part of the food supply in South Asia and Africa. In India, for example, women use up to 150 species of plants as medicine, food or fodder, which would ordinarily be described by the biotechnology industry as weeds. In West Bengal, 124 of so-called 'weed' species collected from rice fields are of economic importance to local farmers (Downes, 2003).

Last but not the least, herbicide-resistant plants systematically destroy the food security of the countries, particularly of developing countries, by establishing the mono-cropping culture deep rooted. In traditional form of agriculture, farmers depend on rotational and mixed-cropping culture to in order to keep the soil healthy and make the field disease-free. But the new GM plants engage the farmers, by luring them with huge profit-promise, in mono-cropping. To get rid of problem of soil infertility and pest attack, chemical fertilizers and pesticides are used. This cropping culture imposes huge debt-burden on the farmers. Thus whenever a crop failure occurs, the farmers commit suicide. The epidemic of farmers' suicide in the Warangal area of Andhra Pradesh, according to Vandana Shiva, can directly be ascribed to the farmers' use of hybrid cotton seeds. Those working on the land in the region, who had traditionally grown pulses, millets and paddy, were lured by seed companies to buy the seeds referred to by the seed merchants as 'white gold', which were supposed to make them millionaires. Instead they became paupers (Downes, 2003).

3.2.2 A Threat to Health Security

The importance of traditional medicines, popularly known as 'alternative medicine' is continuously increasing all over the world. In one of the studies by the World Health Organization (WHO), it is estimated that 80 % of the population of developing countries relies on traditional plant based medicines for their health requirements (WHO, 1991).

With this increasing importance, events of piracy of plants with medicinal values and medicinal knowledge of traditional healers are also on increase at a rapid pace. This trend, on the one hand, seriously challenges health security of the concerned country and, on the other, dampens their prospect of foreign exchange earnings from the export of plants and parts of plants thereof with medicinal values. India, being a mega-diversity hotspot[8] of the world is one among the worst sufferers.

India is considered to be the treasure house of medicinal plant species and also of traditional medicinal knowledge. Although it is very difficult to specify the number of such plant species, rough estimates are always available. The Ministry of Environment and Forest, Government of India has identified and documented over 9,500 species of medicinal plants that are significant for the pharmaceutical industry. Of these, 2000 to 2,300 species are used in traditional medicines while at least 150 species are used commercially on a large scale (EXIM Bank, 1997). According to another estimate, there are about 45,000 medicinal plant species in India, with concentrated spots in the region of Eastern Himalayas, Western Ghats and Andaman and Nicobar Islands (Table 3.1).

The officially documented plants with medicinal potential are 3,000, but traditional practitioners use more than 6,000 (Patro, 2016). In another project report, The All India Coordinated Research Project on Ethno-botany has revealed that the tribal communities have knowledge of the use of over 9,000 plant species. For healing alone, they use over 7,500 species of plants. This figure does not include the number of animals, insects, lichens, fungi, minerals, soils and so forth that are also used for human and veterinary health care (Sahai, 2004).

Table 3.1. Medicinal Plants: Availability and Use.

Region	Medicinal Plants Available so far	Medicinal Plants Used so far
World	250,000	35,000–70,000
China	35,000	10,000–11,250
India	45,000	7,500–8,000

Source: Compiled from different sources.

Owing to this richness in biodiversity[9] and also to her richness in traditional knowledge base of indigenous people, India could be the major exporter of alternative medicines. But the plundering and patenting of medicinal plants and associated knowledge of using the resources by the large MNCs prevent India to be the leader of alternative medicine. The absence of appropriate legal protection mechanism is making India incapable of exploiting this golden opportunity.

Trading of medicinal plants, both in the national and international market, both in terms of value and volume, is increasing at a rapid pace. A study conducted by the National Medicinal Plants Board (NMPB) in collaboration with the Foundation for Revitalization of Local Health Tradition (FRLHT), Bangalore estimated that total traded quantity of medicinal plants in India was about 3.19 lakh metric tonnes for the year 2005–2006. In a recent study by NMPB in collaboration with ICFRE, Dehradun estimated that consolidated commercial demand of herbal raw drugs for the year 2014–2015 stood at 5.12 lakh metric tonnes.

World market of herbal medicine is also increasing rapidly. The last three decades have seen substantial growth in herb and herbal product markets across the world. For example, according to an FAO estimate, total traded value of herbal medicine in the world market in 1994 was 12.4 billion US dollars. The value increased to 19.5 US dollars in1999 and 22.4 US dollars in 2002 (FAO). Rapid growth of trade in medicinal plants can be attributed to worldwide interest in herbal products as well as in traditional health systems. At present, 80% of the population in developing countries relies largely on plant-based drugs for their health care needs, and the WHO has estimated that in coming decades a similar percentage of the world population may well rely on plant-based medicines (FAO). On the other hand, the percentage of people using traditional medicines in developed countries hovers around 50% of total population, e.g., 42% in the United States, 48% in Australia and 49% in France rely on traditional medicine. The major exporters of herbal medicines are some developing countries like China, the Republic of Korea, Chile, India, Brazil and Thailand. Except China all of these countries suffer huge trade deficit every year and thereby always remain in need of foreign exchange. If piracy of medicinal plants and associated knowledge of their use can't be prevented, economies of these countries will definitely suffer a lot.

3.3 CASE HISTORIES OF BIO-PIRACY IN INDIA

India has an age-old civilization. The history of advancement of sciences, especially of medical science, in those days of ancient civilization is well known. The branch of medical science through which this advancement was achieved is known as Ayurveda. Ayurvedic medicines are the fruits of richness of biodiversity[9] of this country along with the scientific insight of the aboriginal communities who, through their keen observation and experiment, discovered the medical properties of various plants and herbs. Unfortunately, this oldest system of medicine of India is now under the threat of bio-pirates. The patent right of neem, turmeric, etc. were already been taken away by the big MNCs. Let us now discuss some such cases of bio-piracy the victim of which is India.

3.3.1 The Case of Turmeric

In 1995, Suman K Das and Harihar P Cohy, on behalf of the University of Mississippi Medical Centre, USA, obtained a patent on the 'use of turmeric in wound healing' from the US patent office. When this event came to the knowledge of the Government of India, a complaint petition was filed by the Council of Scientific Research (CSIR), an autonomous institution under the Department of Science and Technology, Government of India, to the US patent office, challenging the novelty of the said invention. In support of their challenge, the CSIR submitted documents of authenticated translation of some texts written originally in Sanskrit, Urdu and Hindi along with a paper published in the journal of the Indian Medical Association in 1953. After examining all the documents, the US patent office in 1997 upheld India's petition and revoked the patent on the anti-inflammatory applications of turmeric on the ground of absence of novelty.

3.3.2 The Case of Neem

The neem (scientifically known as *Azadirachta indica*) has its native in Africa and South and Southeast Asia, especially in India. Indians described the tree as 'azaddarakht-i-Hindil', which literally means 'the free tree of India' (Lukose, 2009). In some Sanskrit texts, the tree is described as the 'curer of all ailments'. In fact, almost every part of this tree is used either as insect and pest repellant in agriculture, or as human and veterinary medicine, or as toiletries and cosmetics. Such uses of the tree are mentioned in different Indian texts since the ages of Rig-Veda written nearly 3,000 to 4,000 years ago.

In the year 1992, the European Patent Office (EPO) granted a patent to an US-based multi-national company W R Grace on a neem-based product. Thereafter, a number of patents were granted to W R Grace and several other companies on different neem-based products. In 1995, a legal opposition to these patents was filled jointly by the Research Foundation for Science,

Technology and Ecology based in Delhi, the International Federation of Organic Agriculture Movements based in Germany and the Green Party in the European Parliament, Brussels. Their claim was that the fungicidal effect of hydrophobic extracts of neem seeds was known and used for centuries on a broad scale in India, both in Ayurvedic medicine to cure dermatological diseases and in traditional Indian agricultural practice to protect crops from being destroyed by fungal infections. This argument by the plaintiffs clarified that the patents were granted violating at least two statutory requirements of granting a patent, namely novelty and inventive steps.

In defense, the opponent party argued that since this traditional knowledge regarding the use of neem was never published in any academic journal, such knowledge cannot enjoy the privilege of prior art. However, this argument did not make any sense to the judiciary, and finally, in 2005, the four-member panel of the Technical Board of Appeals of the EPO revoked the patents on neem products.

3.4 CASE HISTORIES OF BIO-PIRACY IN OTHER COUNTRIES

Incidents of bio-piracy are not confined to India only. In fact, almost all the developing and underdeveloped countries rich in biodiversity are the victims of bio-piracy. Examples are innumerable. Only a few of them are mentioned below.

3.4.1 The Case of Ayahuasca

An indigenous community of the Amazon rain forest, the Shamans, had been using for centuries a woody vine, popularly known as ayahuasca (means 'wine of the soul'), to prepare a hallucinogenic drink. These drinks are used for treating illnesses and are a part of religious and spiritual ceremonies where they are used to achieve trace states, train future shamans and induce dreams and prophecies (Dobkin and Rumrrill, 2008).

This particular plant was taken patented in 1986 by some Loren Miller. Miller demanded to discover a supposedly new variety of the ayahuasca plant, which he named 'Da Vine'. 'Da Vine' was claimed to be new because of the newness of the colour of the flower. In fact, Miller had found the plant in a domestic garden of Amazon rainforest, but since the indigenous community held no patent for the plant, the United States allowed for Miller to be granted one (Robinson, 2010).

In granting the patent over ayahuasca the US government, in fact, overlooked how the indigenous communities had cultivated the plant over centuries and failed to acknowledge that 'Da Vine' was actually the intellectual property of the indigenous community. A petition was then submitted by The Coalition for Amazonian Peoples and their Environment and the Coordinating Body of Indigenous Organizations of the Amazon Basin with the help of the Centre for International Environmental Law (CIEL) to revoke the patent on the ground that 'Da Vine' was not a new invention, that it had been previously cultivated and that by patenting it, the United States was violating the morality and public policy aspects of the Act (Tupper, 2009).

In 1999 Miller's patent was revoked but only because the same variety was found in Chicago's Field Museum, and not because they took into consideration the indigenous communities' use of the plant (Fecteau, 2001). However, later on the 'Da Vine' patent was reinstated to Miller by allowing him to submit new evidence.

3.4.2 The Case of Enola Bean

The farmers in the north-west of Mexico have long been producing a bean which is an important staple and also an important source of income of them. In 1994 Larry Proctor, a US citizen, collected this seed. He then developed a new variety of this bean from the mother seed. The new variety was different from the original one only in colour. The new variety had a yellow coat. Mr Proctor called the variety 'Enola' and applied for a patent. He was granted a patent in 1999 by the US Patent and Trademark Office (USPTO). The patent was later assigned to his seed company POD-NERS.

The granting of this patent severely hampered the interests of the poor Mexican farmers and the International Center for Tropical Agriculture (CIAT). The CIAT is home to the world's largest bean collection, with over 27,000 accessions of Phaseolus seeds. Of these, 260 are yellow and six fall within the colour spectrum of the patent for 'Enola' bean. It freely distributes yellow beans to plant breeders and researchers from around the world, who regularly access bean samples from its collection (New agriculturist, 2009). Patenting of the yellow bean was prohibiting the CIAT in continuing its programme. The farmers, on the other hand, were no longer been able to sell their crop in the market. An appeal was, therefore, filed by the CIAT in 2000 against the granting of patent to Enola bean. In 2008 the US Board of Patent Appeals and Interferences (BPAI) finally rejected the patent. The POD-NERS then applied to the United States Court of Appeals for the Federal Circuit (CAFC) on July 10, 2009. The Court affirmed the decision of the BPAI to reject all claims for Enola bean. POD-NERS once again petitioned for a panel rehearing which was denied on September 16, 2009 (K Chapman, 2009).

3.5 ACCESS AND BENEFIT SHARING MECHANISM

The concept of Access and Benefit Sharing (ABS) Mechanism has developed in the context of genetic resources and knowledge of indigenous communities relating to these resources. The discussion on this topic started gaining momentum with the introduction of genetic engineering in the field of biotechnology.

Bio-resources have long been used in the pharmaceutical industry. Who, in India, doesn't know the Ayurvedic medicines or Unani therapy? But the problem with these systems of medicine was that their industrial applications were difficult. The genetic engineering opened up a new avenue for these medicines by removing this obstacle.

But the use of genetic engineering in the pharmaceutical industry developed a new threat to the holders of traditional knowledge. Insofar as the traditional medicines were being manufactured manually by the traditional healers themselves, the question of pirating their knowledge didn't arise. Now as soon as the industrial use of traditional knowledge became possible a tendency of bio-piracy, instead of bio-prospecting, started developing.

Bio-prospecting is the process of collecting and using the bio-resources along with the knowledge of their use with due acknowledgment to their original owner. Bio-piracy, on the other hand, is the technique of collecting and using the same unlawfully, without proper acknowledgment. Bio-prospecting is thus a necessary precondition of economic and scientific advancement. The question of access mechanism, which can ascertain the fair use of bio-resources and traditional knowledge, arises here only. If a fair access mechanism can't be developed, incidents of bio-piracy will increase by leaps and bounds.

Access to bio-resources and related knowledge may be of two types. The first one covers transborder access and in this sense is international in character. The second one is domestic in nature and related to accessing traditional knowledge regarding the use of bio-resources.

The issue of access to bio-resources, including genetic resources, was brought into discussion in the international arena, especially by the Convention of Biological Diversity. One of the three main objectives of this Convention, according to Article 1, is the fair and equitable sharing of the benefits arising out of the utilization of genetic resources. Moreover, Article 15 of the Convention addresses the terms and conditions for access to genetic resources and benefit-sharing. First of all, it recognizes the sovereignty of States over their natural resources. It then provides that access to these resources shall be subject to the prior informed consent (PIC) of the resource-provider and shall be based on mutually agreed terms (MAT) in order to ensure the sharing of benefits arising from the commercial or other utilization of these genetic resources.

The issue of access and benefit sharing mechanism started to be discussed first in the fourth Conference of Parties of the CBD. At this meeting in 1998, the Conference of the Parties decided to establish a Panel of Experts on Access and Benefit-sharing to clarify principles and concepts related to ABS. Thereafter, fifth COP established an Ad Hoc Open-ended Working Group on Access and Benefit Sharing comprised of government-nominated representatives and open to participation by indigenous and local communities, non-government organizations (NGOs), industry, scientific and academic institutions, and inter-governmental organizations. Its mandate was to develop guidelines, other approaches and their respective elements to serve as inputs for drafting legislative, administrative or policy measures and contractual arrangements under mutually agreed terms for access and benefit sharing (Tully, 2003). The result of all these initiatives gave birth to Bonn Guidelines in the year 2002.

3.5.1 Bonn Guidelines

The first draft of the Bonn Guidelines on Access to Genetic Resources and the Fair and Equitable Sharing of Benefits Arising out of Their Utilization was prepared in the intergovernmental meeting of the CBD in October 2001 and was eventually adopted, with moderate changes, by the Conference of the Parties to the Convention at its sixth meeting, held in The Hague in April 2002.

The CBD recognized, in line with the PGRFA, the sovereign rights of States over their biological as well as plant genetic resources, and thereby ascribed the authority to determine access to genetic resources to the respective national governments and subject to their national legislation. The objective of Bonn Guidelines, which is voluntary in nature, therefore, was to develop a transparent legal framework for the member countries to the CBD that would ensure a fair and equitable access and benefit sharing mechanism. A framework based only on PIC and MAT can satisfy this objective.

3.5.1.1. Prior Informed Consent

Prior informed consent (PIC) means advance approval of the right holders of genetic resources and the holders of associate knowledge for the use of the resources as well as the knowledge regarding their use. According to Article 15(5) of the Convention on Biological Diversity, access to genetic resources shall be subject to prior informed consent of the contracting Party providing such resources, unless otherwise determined by that Party. In accordance with this Article of the CBD the Bonn Guidelines set the basic principles of a prior informed consent system, which should include the following: (1) legal certainty and clarity; (2) access to genetic resources should be facilitated at minimum cost; (3) restrictions on access to genetic resources should be transparent, based on legal grounds, and not run counter to the objectives of the Convention; and (4) consent of the relevant competent national authority(ies) in the provider country. The consent of relevant stakeholders, such as indigenous and local communities, as appropriate to the circumstances and subject to domestic law, should also be obtained.

According to the Guidelines anyone can apply for the access. But the applicant should (1) specify the quantity and type of resources to be accessed; (2) specify the duration of access activities; (3) specify where and how the research will be carried on; (4) disclose the information about the use and purpose of access; (5) specify the means of benefit sharing mechanism; and (6) specify the types and kinds of the benefits to be accrued from the accesses activities.

The Guideline makes it very clear that the process must be simple and uniform subject to reasonable time bound process.

3.5.1.2. Conditions Relating to Mutually Agreed Terms (MAT)

According to the Guidelines (UNEP, 2002) the following principles could be considered for the development of mutually agreed terms: (1) legal certainty and clarity; (2) minimization of transaction costs; (3) inclusion of provisions on user and provider obligations; (4) development of different contractual arrangements for different resources and for different uses and development of model agreements; (5) different uses may include, inter alia, taxonomy, collection, research and commercialization; (6) mutually agreed terms should be negotiated efficiently and within a reasonable period of time; and (7) mutually agreed terms should be set out in a written agreement.

Moreover the Guidelines speaks of regulating the use of resources in order to take into account ethical concerns of the particular parties and stakeholders, in particular concerned indigenous and local communities. It also proposes to make provision to ensure the continued customary use of genetic resources and related knowledge. The MAT should cover the conditions, obligations, procedures, types, timing, distribution and mechanisms of sharing benefits that arise out of the commercial and other utilization of genetic resources and their derivatives and products. The benefit should be shared fairly and equitably with all those who have contributed to the resource management, scientific and/or commercial process. The Guidelines also specify that the benefit-sharing mechanism should be flexible as it should be determined by the partners involved in benefit-sharing and will vary on a case-by-case basis.

3.5.2 The Nagoya Protocol

The Nagoya Protocol on Access to Genetic Resources and the Fair and Equitable Sharing of Benefits Arising from their Utilization, an international, legally binding framework to promote a transparent and effective implementation of the ABS concept at the regional, national and local level, was adopted in Nagoya, Japan in 2010. It establishes a regulatory framework for accessing genetic resources and/or traditional knowledge associated with genetic resources and sharing the benefits arising from the utilization of such resources and knowledge with the respective stakeholders. It obliges Parties to ensure that users under their jurisdiction respect the domestic ABS legislation and regulatory requirements of the Parties where the resources or knowledge have been acquired (Greiber et al., 2012).

The objective of this Protocol is to ensure access to genetic resources in an appropriate manner and the fair and equitable sharing of the benefits arising from the utilization of these resources. In Article 6, the Protocol says that utilization of genetic resources 'shall be subject to the prior informed consent of the Party providing such resources'. To ensure PIC building up of necessary legislative, administrative or policy has been stressed on (Article 6.3). In fact, in several occasions the Protocol emphasized on building up of necessary legal and administrative structure so that these regulations can be implemented in an appropriate manner.

In regard to 'benefit sharing' the Protocol emphasizes that the benefits that have to be shared should not only be arose from the utilization of genetic resources but also from subsequent applications and commercialization of such resources (Article 5.1). Moreover, such sharing 'shall be upon mutually agreed terms' (Article 5.2). The benefits may, however, be monetary or/and non-monetary.

The Nagoya Protocol supplements the CBD by making provisions for implementation mechanism. The Nagoya Protocol is intended to create greater legal certainty and transparency for both providers and users of genetic resources by establishing core obligations for its contracting parties (Robinson, 2010). In addition to supplementing the CBD these core provisions significantly expands the traditional knowledge and access and benefit-sharing (ABS) provisions of the CBD. In its main ABS provision contained in Article 15, the CBD covers only genetic resources. Unlike genetic resources, the CBD does not proclaim that Parties hold rights to traditional knowledge associated with genetic resources, but it does not exclude this possibility either (Greiber, 2012). While addressing traditional knowledge associated with genetic resources the Protocol states:

> *In implementing their obligations under this Protocol, Parties shall in accordance with domestic law take into consideration indigenous and local communities'*

> *customary laws, community protocols and procedures, as applicable, with respect to traditional knowledge associated with genetic resources.*
>
> (Article 6.1).

Practice of exchanging genetic resources and associated traditional knowledge within and amongst the communities is an age-old practice of aboriginal communities. The CBD recognized that such non-commercial practice should no way be restricted. In line with this view of CBD the Protocol iterates:

> *Parties, in their implementation of this Protocol, shall, as far as possible, not restrict the customary use and exchange of genetic resources and associated traditional knowledge within and amongst indigenous and local communities in accordance with the objectives of the Convention.*
>
> (Article 6.4).

This article, therefore, indirectly mentions that ABS mechanism should be developed only for commercial utilization of genetic resources and associated traditional knowledge.

3.6 EXAMPLES OF ACCESS AND BENEFIT SHARING OVER THE COUNTRIES

Countries rich in bio-resources and in relating traditional knowledge often become victims of misappropriation of this asset base of them. One of the reasons behind such misappropriation is the absence of proper legal structure. When such events happen, the best way is to make formal agreement with the user in regard to sharing the benefits of commercial use of this resource and knowledge base. However, throughout the world of biodiversity-rich countries examples of formal agreement of ABS are scarcely available. A few of the available examples are discussed below.

3.6.1 Examples of Access and Benefit Sharing in India

3.6.1.1. Agreement on Jeevani

The most cited example of benefit sharing in India was agreed upon between Tropical Botanical Garden and Research Institute (TBGRI) and Kerala Kani Samudaya Kshema Trust (KKSKT). The benefit sharing model evolved and experimented by TBGRI has received wide acclaim, acceptance and popularity as it was the first of its kind in the world to recognize and reward the IPR of an indigenous community for sharing their indigenous knowledge that resulted ultimately in the development (Ghose, 2004).

In 1987 an ethno-botanical expedition was being conducted by a team from the All India Coordinated Research Project on Ethnobiology (AICRPE) in the mountainous forests of Western Ghats of Kerala. Dr P. Pushpangadan, Director, National Botanical Research Institute was leading the expedition. He was accompanied by some young people from the 'Kanis', a semi-nomadic forest dwelling tribe.

During the arduous trekking, Pushpangadan observed that these young people on and off were consuming the black fruit of a wild plant. Dr Pushpangadan also observed that after each consumption the boys started working more enthusiastically. When the boys offered this fruit to the exhausted members of the team of scientists, they took it and 'upon eating the fruits, AICRPE team felt immediately charged and full of energy and vitality' (Pushpangadan et al., 1988).

The real story started only thereafter. Dr Pushpangadan and his team members started persuading their guides to disclose the identity of the plant. The tribal boys were initially reluctant on the ground that it was a time-honored tribal secret and a sacred one. But when Dr Pushpangadan were able to convince them that they would try to develop and finally market a drug based on this fruit and share the benefit arising out of this enterprise with their community, they agreed upon.

The plant they then showed to the scientist was called Arogyapacha which was later identified as *Trichopus zeylanicus*[10]. A prolonged scientific investigation (phyto-chemical and ethno-pharmacological) of 7 years on Arogyapacha finally gave birth to a scientifically verified and standardized herbal formulation 'Jeevani' which has profound anti-stress, anti-fatigue and immune-enhancing properties.

In 1996, the manufacturing right of 'Jeevani' was transferred to the Arya Vaidya Pharmacy of Coimbatore against a license fee of Rs. ten lakh and a royalty of two percent at ex-factory sale rate While transferring the technology Tropical Botanical Garden and Research Institute (TBGRI) of Thiruanantapuram agreed to share the licence fee and the royalty received with the Kanis on 1:1 ratio. However, the benefits to the 'Kani' tribe could finally be transferred only after the constitution of 'Kerala Kani Samudaya Kshema Trust'.

3.6.2 Examples of ABS in Other Countries

3.6.2.1. The Case of Hoodia

Hoodia is a succulent plant native to southern Africa. The plant had long been used to stave off hunger and thirst by the indigenous San peoples, the oldest human inhabitants in Africa.

In 1995 the South African-based Council for Scientific and Industrial Research (CSIR) patented the use of the active constituents of the plant responsible for suppressing appetite, without the consent of the San. In 1997 CSIR granted a license for the further development and commercialization of the patent to a UK-based company, Phytopharm. The agreement granted to Phytopharm was an exclusive worldwide license to manufacture and market Hoodia-related products and to exploit any other part of CSIR's IPRs relating to Hoodia (Laird & Wynberg, 2008).

In 2001 *The Observer* reports commercial development of Hoodia without involvement of the San (Wynberg, 2004). When the report reached to the Sans, some members of the community filed a suit against CSIR and the pharmaceutical company Phytopharm on the ground that it was a clear case of bio-piracy and that both the CSIR and Phytopharm violated the terms of PIC and MAT. A negotiation between the CSIR and the San started commencing only thereafter. In 2002 a Memorandum of Understanding was signed between the CSIR and the South African San Council that recognized the San as the originators of knowledge regarding the use of Hoodia and accordingly included a commitment to share the benefits, the details of which would decided to be finalized later. The agreement finally reached in 2003 stated that

> *...the San would receive 6% of all royalties received by the CSIR from Phytopharm for products and 8% of milestone income when certain targets were reached. Money was to be paid into a trust set up jointly by the CSIR and the South African San Council "to raise the standard of living and well-being of San peoples of southern Africa". Strict rules were developed to distribute the funds. Since the knowledge about the plant was held collectively by the San community, the San representatives came to an agreement that the money would be shared between all southern Africa's San.*
>
> (Wynberg, 2004).

3.6.2.2. The Case of INBio-Merck Agreement

It was in the year 1991, an agreement regarding access and benefit sharing between Costa Rica's non-profit private organization National Biodiversity Institute (INBio) and one of the largest pharmaceutical MNCs Merck had drawn international attention. This agreement was, in fact, the first ever attempt of commercializing genetic and biological resources of a country with proper benefit sharing. In this agreement, a temporary right to perform pharmacological analysis of genetic resources as well as the right to patent the developed drugs was granted to Merck.

By the agreement INBio confirmed to provide Merck with (1) a limited number of plants, insect and environmental samples for pharmaceutical and agricultural applications for an initial period of 2 years (Merck & Co., Inc, 1993) and (2) facilities for the collection and processing of biological samples.

On the other hand, Merck, in turn, agreed to provide (1) training of INBio staff at Merck facilities; (2) US $1 million during the agreement's two-year period for research; (3) laboratory equipment worth US $130000 for use at the University of Costa Rica and (4) royalties on the sale of any pharmaceutical products that Merck brings to market as a result of an INBio sample or compound (INBio, 1991).

This agreement between Merck and INBio is considered as a model agreement of benefit sharing in cases of bio-prospecting. Inbio developed a few more agreements like this with some other organizations. But in practice, INBio's deal with Merck and other bio-prospecting contracts failed to generate enough revenue for the Institute to make them economically viable (Hammond, 2015).

4

PROTECTING TRADITIONAL KNOWLEDGE: WAYS AND MEANS

4.1 WHAT IS INTELLECTUAL PROPERTY?

Intellectual property (IP) is an intangible one. Intellect is nothing but the power of brain of a person. Hence it is an intangible asset. According to World Intellectual Property Organization (WIPO) 'intellectual property refers to creations of the mind: inventions; literary and artistic works; and symbols, names and images used in commerce'.

Intellectual property is divided into two categories, namely industrial property and copyright. Industrial property includes patents for inventions, trademarks, industrial designs and geographical indications. Copyright, on the other hand, covers literary works (such as novels, poems and plays), films, music, artistic works (e.g., drawings, paintings, photographs and sculptures) and architectural design.

4.2 PROTECTING INTELLECTUAL PROPERTY RIGHT

The right to intellectual property must go in favour of the person who possesses it. But the problem is that how can an asset be protected by the law which is beyond tangibility? In fact, this is an impossible task. So what we usually do in such cases is that we protect the fruits of the intellect, instead of protecting the intellect itself. For example, we extend protection to the invention of a scientist, the writings of an author, instead of protecting the intellect of the author or the scientist. Therefore, protecting intellectual property right (IPR) means extending a right to the inventor/creator for his/her invention/creation. This right will enable the right-holder to get benefit from the production and sale of his/her invention/creation.

However, an individual cannot enjoy the right over his/her intellectual property for an indefinite period. According to WTO 'intellectual property rights are the rights given to persons over the creations of their minds for a certain period of time'. However, this time period may vary from country to country. In fact, before the commencement of WTO in 1995, there was no unique period of time for which this right was granted in different countries. But the TRIPS agreement of WTO has fixed this time period which would be applicable to all the member countries of WTO.

There are several laws relating to intellectual property right protection, namely, Patent Law, Trademark Law, Geographical Indication Act, Industrial Design Act, Copyright Act, etc. However, here we restrict our discussion only with those laws which are or which may be used in protecting traditional knowledge (TK).

4.3 ALTERNATIVE WAYS TO PROTECT TRADITIONAL KNOWLEDGE

Extending protection to TK holders need to satisfy two conditions. First one is to uphold the rights of the TK holders. The other one is to prevent unauthorized appropriation of the TK. Therefore, two forms of protection have been developed and applied (WIPO, Booklet 2):

1. Positive protection: giving TK holders the right to take action or seek remedies against certain forms of misuse of TK;
2. Defensive protection: safeguarding against illegitimate IP rights taken out by others over TK subject matter.

These two approaches have their own advantages and disadvantages and none is proved to be full-proof. Stakeholders, therefore, have emphasized that these two approaches should be undertaken in a complementary way. A comprehensive approach to the protection of the interests of the TK holders is unlikely to rely totally on one form or the other (WIPO, Booklet).

4.3.1 Positive protection

The rights of TK holders, right now, all over the world, are being protected mainly by means of different types of existing IP laws. Except IP laws, various non-IP options are also available. The non-IP options include trade practices and labelling laws, the law of civil liability, the use of contracts, customary laws[11] and other legislative measures and indigenous laws of the concerned country. Some countries again have enacted *sui generis* law for the protection of the TK. However, many countries are still undecided and have argued that the form of protection should refer to collective human rights to protect their distinct identities; religious and cultural heritage. Others are waiting for the regional or international instruments to protect their TK (Wekundah, 2012).

Although different IP laws are used to protect the rights of TK holders, none of them can completely address the needs and expectations of the traditional communities. Among the various IPR laws which are extensively used to protect TK are laws of patent, trademarks, geographical indications, industrial designs and trade secrets. In a subsequent section, we shall analyze these laws and try to point the limitations of these laws out to protect the interests of the traditional, indigenous communities.

4.3.2 Defensive protection

Defensive protectionist policy aims to protect TK from misappropriation. Misappropriation of TK is taking place mainly through getting patent right of a product which uses the TK. Novelty is one of the basic criteria of getting patent right. When determining whether a claim is novel the prior art base (the public domain) is examined. If the invention or claim is found described in the prior art base, or offered for use or sale for more than one year, it is not entitled to a patent (Hansen & Vanfleet, 2003).

Defensive protection policy wants to use this clause of the Patent Act to prevent the bio pirates from misappropriating TK. This can be done by documenting TK and making it public. Documentation intentionally made available to the public as prior art in order to render any subsequent claims of invention or discovery ineligible for a patent. A defensive disclosure provides evidence of the invention, knowledge or use of the invention by others before it was claimed by another inventor, or offers evidence of public use or sale more than one year before the filing date of the patent (Pryor, 1991).

The main difference between positive protection and defensive protection is that where positive protection guarantees legal protection to the right of TK holders, defensive protection does not. Defensive protection can only help a country to fight against bio-piracy. If a country takes the resort of defensive disclosure it would be difficult for the patent authority of another country to grant patent to a product which is based on the TK of the country who already brought it to the public domain. Moreover, even if such a patent is somehow granted it would be much easier for the country, who already disclosed its traditional knowledge base, to invalidate the patent with relatively little up-front costs.

There is one more important difference between positive protection and defensive protection. Since positive protection provides legal instrument to protect the interest of the TK holders it, besides extending legal protection, also ensures the sharing of benefits arising out of the commercial use of the TK. The question of benefit sharing does not arise in case of defensive disclosure because this does not provide any legal instrument.

There are basically two types of mechanisms to defensively disclose information. One consists of the traditional methods of publication in scientific, academic, technical and business journals, etc. The other is the disclosure via developing a digital database or via electronic media like internet.

One of the most important vehicles for defensive disclosure is a community registry, such as traditional knowledge registries. A traditional knowledge registry, if it is 'public' in nature, places information in the public domain and serve as a form of prior art or defensive disclosure. Traditional knowledge registries[12] are official collections of documentation that describe traditional knowledge. It is typically kept in the form of a computer database. However, a huge risk is associated in building such a digital library. In the absence of any global safeguards, the digital library will become a much wanted source of information on bio-prospecting for private companies. If such digital libraries are constructed all over the world, private companies will surely laugh their way to the bank (Sharma, 2002).

4.4 POSITIVE PROTECTION VIA INTELLECTUAL PROPERTY RIGHTS LAWS

Positive protection provides protection to traditional knowledge with the help of legal weapons. Some such weapons are discussed bellow.

4.4.1 Patent

The most widely used weapon in protecting intellectual property rights is known as patent. Patent has an age-old history, dating back to about the thirteenth century. It is actually a monopoly right granted to an inventor for his invention. The monopoly right is meant mainly for commercial production and sale of the invented product. This right may be used by the inventor himself or by his agent or by anyone else to whom a license of using the right has been issued by the inventor.

In fact, during initial periods of industrial revolution in the United Kingdom, newer and newer machines were being invented frequently. But whenever a new machine came into the market, it was soon copied, sometimes even before the inventor could recover his cost of research and development. The idea of providing some kind of protection in the form of granting an exclusive right of using his invention came as a result. The objective was to ensure a satisfactory amount of return to the inventor and by this way to give a boost to him for further research and development.

The grant of an exclusive right of using an invention to its inventor appeared for the first time in the thirteenth century and was quite frequent in the fourteenth. However, at that time what was given was not a formal patent right, nor was it given only to the first and true inventor. Actually manufacturing monopolies or licensing monopolies were given either to a producer introducing a technology already used abroad or to the first and true inventor.

Patents for inventions only were introduced in the fifteenth century in certain Italian states. The first of its kind was granted in the Republic of Florence in 1421. During the first one or two centuries, these grants were ordinarily made without any specific statutes on the subject, but by the virtue of the general authority and the power of the ruler. In 1474, an ordinance relating to patents was enacted in Venice. But formal, comprehensive patent statutes did not appear until near the close of the eighteenth century. It first appeared in the United States in 1790.

An attempt to build an international treaty on patent right was made first in 1873 when a discussion was initiated at Vienna, Austria. But no consensus could be reached. Thereafter, a treaty, known as International Union for the Protection of Industrial Property was finally arrived at the Paris Convention in 1883. But only 14 countries signed it initially. Still this Convention has a special importance in the history of patent laws. The importance lies in the fact that even the non-member countries of the Paris Convention build their own patent laws up on the basis of the provisions mentioned in the Paris Convention (Balasubramaniam, 1987).

4.4.2 Plant Patent

The protection to plant genetic resources was first sought by the United States in the late 1920s. After the World War I, the

US government found it difficult to put more investment in the agricultural sector through public sectors. The government of the United States, therefore, took decision in promoting and encouraging the participation of the private sector in the field of agriculture (Elumalai, 2012). This policy decision led the US government to enact the Plant Patenting Act in the year 1930. The objective was to give incentive to private corporate bodies in the development of high-yielding varieties (HYV) seeds in their laboratories. In fact, the research towards developing HYV seeds started during this period. Attracted by the lucrative profit-prospect of seed business private corporate bodies of the United States put pressure on their government to ensure the signing of an international treaty which would recognize the breeders' right on these newly developed seeds. The International Convention for the Protection of New Varieties of Plants (the UPOV convention) was signed by 12 developed countries in 1961 in Paris as the fall out of this corporate pressure. In contrary to this UPOV convention, the Food and Agriculture Organization (FAO) in its 1983 Undertaking declared plant genetic resources to be the common heritage of mankind.

4.4.3 Geographical Indication

Geographical indicator (GI) is such an indicator which helps us to identify the geographical origin of a product. The quality and characteristics of the product are exclusively or essentially derived from the geographical environment, including natural and human factors (Suh & MacPherson, 2007). The WTO, in its agreement on TRIPS (Article 22) defines GIs as 'indications which identify a good as originating in the territory of a member, or a region or locality in that territory, where a given quality, reputation or other characteristic of the good is essentially attributable to its geographical origin'. For example, Darjeeling Tea is the geographical indication of varieties of tea that are produced in the district of Darjeeling, West Bengal, India and its surrounding areas. The flavour for which Darjeeling Tea acquired its worldwide reputation is derived from the climatic condition of the area.

A particular good comes to be known by its place of origin only when it earns some kind of reputation. Geographical indications, therefore, have immense commercial potential. Owing to this potentiality GIs often become the victim of piracy. The famous example in this regard is the case of Basmati. Protection to the products with geographical specialty is, therefore, essential, on the one hand, to keep them away from being pirated and, on the other, to exploit their commercial potentiality by the original owner.

The idea of exploiting the specialty of a product arising out of its regional character can be traced back in the seventeenth century, when some European countries wanted to develop a mechanism that could protect the commercial interest of their traders who had acquired some reputation in the international market for the specialty of their product, originated due to their spatial character. The case for geographical indication was first discussed in the Paris Convention for the Protection of Industrial Property (1883). Later on the issue of protecting GI was agreed on the Madrid Agreement for the Repression of False or Deceptive Indications of Source on Goods (1891) and the Lisbon Agreement for the Protection of Appellations of Origin and their International Registration (1958).

4.4.4 Copyright

Copyright, a kind of intellectual property right, confers to the creator, author or the artist, an exclusive right over their creations like musical composition, film; literary works like books and articles; and artistic works like paintings, drawings, sculpture, etc.

The idea of copyright protection emerged with the invention of printing, which made the literary works to be duplicated by mechanical process (Dureja, 2015). The Gutenberg's printing press was discovered in Germany in 1436. But the first legal attempt to protect copyright was taken only in 1662, when the Licensing Act was passed in England. This Act, titled 'An Act for preventing the frequent abuses in printing seditious, treasonable and unlicensed Books and Pamphlets and for regulating of Printing and Printing Presses', prohibited the printing of any book which was not licensed and registered with the Stationers Company. The Stationers' Company, in fact, was a guild of printers and publishers. Queen Mary I of England, who was becoming more and more unpopular to her people, granted this exclusive right to this company in order to censor, in the name of protecting copyright and checking piracy, any kind of propaganda against her governance. This Act, therefore, in practice, protected the copyright of the publishers, not of the authors. Only the authors, who were pro-queen and the books of whom were selected by the Company for publication, enjoyed copyright over their books.

The first ever codified, comprehensive law which upheld the copyright of the authors was enacted in 1710 by Queen Anne. This Act is known as the Statute of Anne or the Copyright Act 1710. The stated objectives of this law, besides protecting copyright of the authors, were the encouragement of learning, spread of knowledge and preservation of knowledge. This Statute conferred a copyright term of 14 years, which could be renewed for a similar term. After the expiration of the copyright the material would fall into public domain. After the introduction of the Statute of Anne, copyright laws, in some form or the other, started to be enacted by different countries of the world. Although almost all of them were following the basic structure set up by the Statute of Anne, there was no uniformity in them and no coordination was seen among the countries. But this coordination was very much essential in the sense that literary and artistic works always have a universal appeal. Hence the rights of a creator can be protected in true sense only when he/she gets uniform protection all over the world. This demands coordination among countries in formulating uniform Copyright Acts. This coordination was finally brought by the Berne Convention.

The Berne Convention for the Protection of Literary and Artistic Works, started in 1886 and completed in 1896, discussed various issues of copyrights at length. The Berne Union, constituted by the member countries of the Convention established minimum standards of protection between signatory states.

The biggest change that was brought by the Berne Convention was the introduction of copyright to the unpublished works (Article 5.2). Beforehand, according to the Statute of Anne, a work would be entitled to get copyright protection only after registering his work with the Stationers' Company. The Berne Convention extended automatic protection to any cultural expression once it was created.

The two other important features of Berne Convention are national treatment and independence. By Article 5(3), the Convention ensures that any work originating in a member state receive the same treatment whether the author is domestic or foreign national. Article 5(1) states that each member state shall extend by their own domestic law, which will be independent of protection extended by other countries to the same work.

The Convention set a term of protection which was the life of the author plus 50 years. However this should be the minimum term. Any country, if it wishes, however, can set a much longer term. India, as a signatory of the Berne Convention, initially, in her Copyright Act of 1957, fixed 50 years as the term of protection. But in 1992, in an amendment to the present Copyright Act, the Government of India extended the term to 60 years. This was done mainly to offer an extra term of protection to the literary works of Rabindranath Tagore. However, it was done in tune with the Berne Convention. While setting the minimum term of protection the Convention also stated that the member countries were free to provide greater term of protection.

Like the Berne Convention, the TRIPS Agreement also discussed the issue of copyright at length (Part II, Section 1). It sets forth certain standards for the protection of authors, broadcasting organizations, performers and phonogram producers. The Agreement opines that 'copyright protection shall extend to expressions and not to ideas, procedures, methods of operation or mathematical concepts as such' (Article 9.2).

4.4.5 Trademark

Trademark bears the identity of a product in the market place as well as in the psychological state of the consumers. In this sense, it gives some kind of protection to the producer/seller of the product because the used-to consumers of the product gradually become familiar with the trademark and in ultimate course show a little bit reluctance to use products of other brand.

By definition, a trademark is a symbol or sign in the form of a word, a label or a device which enables the producers/sellers to make their product easily distinguishable and identifiable from similar goods and services supplied by the others.

Trademark, a mark of identity, can, therefore, be regarded as a beneficiary mark for trade. This mark, in fact, started its journey during the tenth Century. Referred to as merchants mark, it was used to prove ownership rights of goods. But trademarks came into prominence during the late eighteenth and early nineteenth centuries with the advent of mass scale production in the industrial sector. During this period, the introduction of mechanical system in the industrial sector, along with almost regular inventions in the field of science and technology, popularly known as industrial revolution, led to profound changes in economic structures. Competition among firms for larger share of market led to the use of distinguishing marks to assist consumers in choosing their preferred products.

Gradually, as industrial revolution had advanced, need for the enactment of a law for regularization and standardization of market competition kicked off. Accordingly, the first statutory enactment in this regard took place in Britain in the year 1875.

The British Trademark Act of 1875 provided for a formal registration of trademark based on the fulfillment of criterion whether the Trademark distinguished the goods of the trader or not. Thus, Registration was considered prima facie evidence of ownership of a Trademark. Eventually, the Trademark Act, 1875 was repealed and substituted by the Patents, Designs and Trademark Act, 1883 which included the facility to register 'fancy words not in common use' and 'brands' as new marks for the first time. This Act was further substituted by the Trademark Act, 1905. The next re-enactment was the Trademark Act, 1938 (Shirolikar, 2011).

4.4.6 Trade Secrets

'Trade secrets' as defined by WIPO, is 'any confidential business information which provides an enterprise a competitive edge'. Trade secrets include both manufacturing and commercial secrets like production technique, compilation method or anything else which have commercial value. Any information, by the Article 39 of the TRIPS agreement, is considered to be secret if (1) it has commercial value; (2) it has been subject to reasonable steps by the owner up the information to keep it secret; and/or (3) it is generally unknown among, or readily accessible to, circles that normally deal with the kind of information in question.

Unlike other forms of intellectual property for the protection of trade secrets no registration is required. A trade secret can get protection for an unlimited period of time until the right-holder is able to maintain the secrecy. Trade secrets do not have any legal protection. Since the property right to trade secret is enjoyed through contractual agreements compensation for the loss of secrecy can be asked for only in cases of breach of contract, breach of confidence and dishonest commercial practices. This means that the right-holder must be able to prove some form of malicious intent on the part of a contracting party as the cause for a trade secret's diffusion to the public.

Generally, trade secret protection is weak in most of the countries, including India. There is no particular legislation to protect undisclosed information outside the normal recourse to breach of contract. Under the Indian contract law, trade secrets usually fall under the ambit of agreements in restraint of profession and trade.

The Government of India introduced the National Innovation Bill in 2008. The Bill has dealt with a number of aspects related to trade secrets such as obligation of confidentiality, remedies to protect confidentiality and damages for violation of trade secrets. The bill, however, did not become a law. Recently National IPR Policy has raised a ray of hope as one of the objectives of the policy is to enact a trade secret law.

4.5 DEFENSIVE PROTECTION

Defensive protection emphasises on the preservation of traditional knowledge. Preservation of TK, according to WIPO, means identification, documentation, transmission, revitalization and promotion of cultural heritage to ensure its maintenance. Preservation of TK, however, implies preservation of both codified and non-codified knowledge. Codified knowledge refers to the knowledge of indigenous communities which are recorded either in any ancient texts or in any contemporary books, journals and reports that focus on TK. Non-codified knowledge, on the other hand, refers to knowledge which exists in oral form only. The Traditional Knowledge Digital Library of India, Traditional Chinese Medicine (TCM) Database of China and The Korean Traditional Knowledge Portal (KTKP) of Korea are examples of digital database of codified TK. They are discussed in Section 4.5.1 and 4.5.2. Documentation of non-codified TK is quite difficult and hence rare. Still countries like Venezuela, South Africa took initiatives in documenting non-codified TK. Such efforts are discussed in Section 4.5.3 (Table 4.1).

4.5.1 Documentation of Codified Traditional Knowledge in India

India is rich in biodiversity, and she also possesses a rich knowledge base in using this bio-resources. But, unfortunately, owing to the lack of proper awareness, this knowledge base was being misappropriated by the multi-national companies of the North. To prevent such bio-piracy, various initiatives are being taken place at the governmental as well as non-governmental level.

Table 4.1. Positive Versus Defensive Protection.

Issues	Post-grant Opposition	Pre-grant
Nature	Opposing party can submit counter documents and participate in re-examination and hearing process.	Objecting party can only file evidence and cannot participate in the examination process.
Cost	Highly expensive, requires legal assistance.	Inexpensive, no requirement of legal support because prior art evidence is available from databases, like Traditional Knowledge Digital Library (TKDL).
Time period	4–13 years	3–20 weeks

4.5.1.1. The Traditional Knowledge Digital Library

Traditional Knowledge Digital Library (TKDL) of India is a knowledge registry. It is actually a digital database of traditional system of medicine in India. Although TK can assume different forms, in building TKDL only the knowledge which can provide important clues to the development of modern drugs thereby saving the time and money is considered. This is due to the increased demand for the traditional medicines all over the world in recent decades. Over 80% of people from developing countries depend on traditional medicines for health needs. A study reveals that even in the developed World a significant percentage of people, for example, 50% in the United States, 75% in France and 90% in the United Kingdom, consume traditional medicine at least once (Venkataraman & Latha, 2008).

The TKDL is a collaborative project between the Council of Scientific and Industrial Research (CSIR) and the Department of Ayurveda, Yoga and Naturopathy, Unani and Siddha and Homeopathy (AYUSH). This digital library contains information on some 22, 60,000 medicinal formulations. The details of these formulations include description, method on the preparation, claim and the usage to make them compatible with the Patent Application Format (Varkay, 2007). Since most of these formulations were originally expressed in languages such as Sanskrit, Arabic, Persian, Urdu and Tamil, which are beyond recognition of the patent examiners working in the major patent offices all over the world, they were translated into English, French, German, Japanese, Spanish and Hindi. The local names of plants were converted into botanical names and Ayurvedic description of diseases into modern medical terminology.

The TKDL was built up on the expectation that it would henceforth help patent authorities to reject a patent application which is based on any Indian TK (Bhukta, 2017). The government therefore decided to sign a TKDL Access Agreement which has built-in, non-disclosure mechanisms to safeguard India's interest and counter any possible misuse. Such a decision was taken initially in the first meeting of the Inter-Ministerial Access Policy Issue Committee on TKDL, held on 20 December 2002. In the meeting, it was decided that the database of the TKDL may be provided to the patent offices of different countries if and only if they sign non-disclosure agreement (NISCAIR, 2003). Under TKDL Access Agreement, patent examiners may use the TKDL for search and examination purposes only and contents may only be revealed to third parties for the purposes of citation[13]. Owing to such an agreement the TKDL has gained the characteristic of neither being a public registry nor a private registry.

The TKDL has succeeded in preventing the grant of quite a large number of patent applications relating to Indian medicinal system. India's success generates initiatives in other countries to build up similar database. The mention may be made in this regard towards the Chinese and Korean initiatives.

4.5.1.2. Other Initiatives of Documenting Traditional Knowledge in India

TKDL is not the only initiative which documented traditional knowledge of India. Several other initiatives are taken by some NGOs and also by few Indian States.

The leading NGOs in India, who play important roles in documenting codified and non-codified TK are Gene Campaign, Society for Research and Initiatives for Sustainable Technologies and Institutions (SRISTI), Kerala Shastra Sahitya Parishad (KSSP), Research Foundation of Science, Technology and Ecology (RFSTE), Navdanya, Kalpavriksh, Beej Bachao Aandolan, etc.

Gene campaign has documented biodiversity and associated indigenous knowledge in Jharkhand, Madhya Pradesh and Uttarakhand. It has focused on three tribal populations: the Munnars in the Chotanagpur region of Jharkhand; the Bhils of Madhya Pradesh; and the Tharus of the Terai region of Uttarakhand. Department of Science and Technology of Indian government supported the documentation. In addition to the collection of information on indigenous knowledge, the project also involved making these communities aware of the threat of bio-piracy, and the implications of IPRs and various national and international developments concerning the protection of biodiversity and indigenous knowledge. Medicinal plants and knowledge related thereto was sought to be documented with the help of educated tribal youth. In this process of documentation, the collection and understanding of the information has been done with the consultation with the medical practitioners, the traditional healers and the elders in the village (Hirwade & Hirwade, 2012).

Research Foundation of Science, Technology and Ecology (RFSTE) along with Navdanya initiated a movement in early 1999 called the Jaiv Panchayat. Activists from RFSTE and Navdanya constituted informal community-level institutions in different villages of India, called Jaiv Panchayats, to prepare traditional knowledge register of the concerned village. The first Jaiv Panchayat to complete such a register was in Agasthyamuni village, Garhwal district, Uttar Pradesh.

SRISTI, an Ahmedabad-based NGO, initiated a documentation network at the village level, known as Honeybee Network, which documents the elements of biodiversity as well as their uses. This network has been growing since the late 1980s.

Beej Bachao Aandolan, a NGO, in collaboration with another NGO Kalpavriksh, initiated the documentation of the various bio resources used by the villagers in Jardhar of the Tehri-Garhwal district of UP and also of their conservation practices. It was decided that the register developed by this initiative can be used and distributed only with the consent and knowledge of the villagers.

The states like Andhra Pradesh, Kerala and Karnataka also took initiatives in promoting village wise Community Biodiversity Registers (CBRs) and People's Biodiversity Registers (PBRs) for documenting all knowledge innovations and practices of local indigenous people. For example, in Kerala one pilot project has been completed in Ernakulum district, in which NGO Kerala Shastra Sahitya Parishad played an instrumental role.

Among the other states of India Kerala deserves the special mention because it developed an IPR policy to protect the traditional knowledge base of the state in the year 2008. Kerala had, in the past, lost several of its traditional knowledge rights on healthcare, food and food supplements, as well as on designs and cultural properties, because the original inventors or communities that inherited the knowledge over generations were not supported by the government. The policy, therefore, outlines the initiatives of the State in protecting her entire traditional knowledge base that consists of knowledge on biodiversity, on tribal medicines and Ayurveda practices (Kuriakose, 2010).

4.5.2 Traditional Knowledge Databases of Other Countries

Inspired by India several, other countries like China and Korea also took initiatives to create their own traditional database. Mention can be made of their initiatives in this regard.

4.5.2.1. Traditional Chinese Medicine Database

China is one of the most TK-rich countries of the world. The most important type of TK in China is Chinese traditional medicine (TCM), derived from ancient traditions and most of it is written down. China has developed a series of online databases containing information on traditional Chinese medicine. The series includes The Traditional Chinese Medicine Database System, The Traditional Chinese Medical Literature Analysis, Traditional Chinese Drug Database, The Database of Chinese Medical Formula and The China Traditional Chinese Medicine Patent Database (CTCMPD).

The Traditional Chinese Medicine Database System was set up by the Institute of Information on TCM. The database consists of over 40 categories of Chinese Medicine Databases, possessing 1,100,000 items most of which are available in Chinese language and a very few in English.

The Traditional Chinese Medical Literature Analysis and Retrieval Database in Chinese contains more than 6,00,000, of which 120,000 are also in English version, references and abstracts to literature on TCM, including Chinese herbal medicines, acupuncture, qigong, Chinese massage, health promotion and other topics. The information is collected since 1984 from different Chinese biomedical journals (Poorna, Mymoon, & Hariharan, 2014).

Traditional Chinese Drug Database in Chinese contains over 11,000 records, 545 of which in English version, with each record representing a single herb, or mineral drug or other natural medicine, and provides the cited information. The data are derived from Chinese Material Medical Dictionary, Thesaurus of Chinese Herbs, Chinese Medicinal Materials, Manual of Composition and Pharmacology of Common Traditional Chinese Medicine, etc.

The Database of Chinese Medical Formula is available only in Chinese and contains information on more than 85,000 medical formulae derived from more than 700 ancient medical books. The Medical News Database in Chinese contains more than 60,000 records of news drawn from newspapers related to Chinese medicine.

The China TCM Patent Database (CTCMPD) was established by Patent Data Research and Development Center (PDC), a part of The Intellectual Property Publishing House of State Intellectual Property Office (SIPO) of China. The original purpose of creating this database was to meet the increasing need of patent examination. The CTCMPD has collected available information on all aspects of drugs including development, synthesis, evaluation, manufacture and applications. This database contains 12,024 deeply indexed records of China TCM patent literature with 31,283 TCM formulas in Chinese. The entire database has been translated into English.

4.5.2.2. The Korean Traditional Knowledge Portal

The Korean Intellectual Property Office (KIPO) decided in 2004 to formulate information strategy planning for the building of a database of traditional knowledge. The database, which was compiled between 2005 and 2007, is based on traditional Korean medicine. The KTKP database is basically an integrated system of content specific databases such as article, herb, prescription, disease databases and other supporting databases; all being interlinked to each other. When a user searches for particular disease-related information, the information on the disease along with related herbs and prescriptions is displayed. Related patents and articles are also provided as separate links (Poorna et al., 2014). The search service of the database started commencing from December 2007. The KTKP database, which is available in Korean and English languages, contains around 3, 50,000 entries on Korean medicine, traditional food and intangible cultural heritage. The KTKP preserves only the codified knowledge and defensively protects Korea's TK.

4.5.3 Documentation of Non-codified Traditional Knowledge: Initiatives in Different Countries

Initiatives for developing database for non-codified traditional knowledge are very limited in number. BioZulua Project of Venezuela and Ulwazi Programme of Durban are two examples.

4.5.3.1. BioZulua Project of Venezuela

Misappropriation of traditional medicinal resources of indigenous Venezuelan communities in the Amazonian forests provoked the Venezuelan authorities in 2002 to launch a new project, named BioZulua project, to safeguard the resource base. The objective was to obtain data about medicinal plants and food crops provided by the 24 ethnic groups living in Venezuelan part of the Amazonian jungle. The database includes information and data on traditional indigenous medicine and traditional technologies pertaining to agriculture, nutrition, conservation practices, etc (Muller, 2004).Under the project, information collected by field researchers will be stored in a database, which will be administered from Caracas by the Foundation for Development of Mathematics and Physical and Natural Sciences (Down to Earth, 2002). The database provides genetic profiles of every plant entry and the entries are complemented with geographical references, bibliographies and digital images. The Biozulua database, however, is not available for public access and has been kept undisclosed for possible positive legal protection through a *sui generis* system in the future (Poorna et al., 2014).

4.5.3.2. Ulwazi Programme of Durban

The Ulwazi Programme was established in 2008 as the first digital library in South Africa aimed at collecting and sharing indigenous knowledge and culture in the greater Durban area in English and local Zulu languages. The Ulwazi Programme collects and shares local knowledge in the form of a 'wiki', a website designed to enable contributions and modifications from multiple users. Local knowledge is recorded on the wiki by fieldworkers who are employed by the programme. The fieldworkers have strong ties to their communities and have been trained in recording audio and visual material, as well as in basic writing and computer skills necessary for the uploading of stories to the wiki[14].The wiki model also encourages the people connected with Durban to register and help improving the database by editing and adding articles. The content is organized through a series of categories and sub-categories (Poorna et al., 2014).

5

INITIATIVES TO PROTECT TRADITIONAL KNOWLEDGE

5.1 INTRODUCTION

Traditional knowledge (TK) all over the world is being protected primarily by the existing intellectual property right (IPR) laws like Copyright Act, Patent Act, Geographical Indications Act, etc. But it was recognized in different occasions in different international fora that the existing legal structure cannot provide proper and sufficient protection to the rights of TK holders. The problem becomes more complicated when the TK is associated with biological resources, because biological matters are beyond protectable under the pre-existing legal structure regarding intellectual property. The WTO, in Article 27.3(b), therefore, categorically stated that the countries may develop their own *sui generis* system in regard to plant variety protection. In protecting TK, particularly those associated with bio-resources, these *sui generis* systems may play important role. In the present chapter, we shall discuss in brief the existing IPR laws which are often used to protect TK along with some newly developed *sui generis* law.

5.2 INITIATIVES IN INDIA

India enacted different IPR laws in different times. The oldest among them is the Patent Act. However, most other IPR laws, except Copyright Act, which are often used as the legal shield against misappropriation of TK, are enacted only after the TRIPS agreement came into force. Some such Acts relevant to the protection of traditional knowledge are discussed in this section.

5.2.1 Patent Act of India

The draft of a Patent Act was first drawn in the Paris Convention in the year 1883. But the first patent law of India was enacted even before the Paris Convention. It was in the year 1856. Thereafter, we have seen several patent laws in our country, e.g. The Patents and Designs Protection Act (1872), The Protection of Inventions Act (1883), Inventions and Designs Act (1888) and The Indian Patents and Designs Act (1911). All these Acts, however, were enacted in the pre-independence period. After independence, several other laws were enacted which tried to protect IPRs.

5.2.1.1. The Indian Patents and Designs Act 1911

The Indian Patents and Designs Act 1911 had a close simile with the Paris Convention draft. This was, however, quite natural. Paris Convention was drafted by industrialized countries. The British, the then ruler of India, normally had an interest in this draft. But India, being an underdeveloped country, had a very different interest from that of the developed industrialized world. So, the interest of the Indian nation was not served by the 1911 Act.

The main argument of the developed countries in formulating patent laws is that if the interest of an innovator cannot be protected by such a law, he will eventually lose interest in further innovation and it will have a dampening effect on the advancement of civilization itself. This is truly a totally misleading argument. Let us explain.

The Paris Convention argued in favour of granting product patent. Patent can normally be granted in two ways: product and process. If product patent is granted for an innovation, no one can produce the same product, even in alternative methods, for the entire period for which the right is granted. On the other hand, granting of process patent means any person can produce the patented product in an alternative method, the method which is not mentioned by the patentee in his patent application. Clearly, process patent tries to serve the interests of both the inventor and the society simultaneously, while the product patent cannot. This is so because once a product patent is granted for a certain period of time, nobody can produce the same for the entire period. This also implies that nobody should be interested in developing a better model of the same until the monopoly period is over, i.e. for the entire patent period, no research will take place in the direction in which a product is already patented. Thus, the basic argument for granting patent right, as it is mentioned by the developed countries, gets rejected automatically if product patent is granted. Since the Paris Convention recommended the granting of the same, its recommendation can be considered as misleading and self-contradictory. Moreover, it is clear from the above discussion that the longer the period of protection, the more is the period for which the human race has to wait for new research and development. Though the Paris Convention did not mention the time period for which patent right can be given, most of the developed countries fixed quite a lengthy period, generally not less than a decade. The intention of the developed world will be very clear from this discussion. These countries were actually very keen to protect the interests of the private innovators and, thereby, to neglect the interests of the common people. Unfortunately, the Indian Patents and Designs Act 1911 contained all of these regulations which were anti-people, anti-development and did not serve the interests of an underdeveloped country.

The 1911 Act provided patent right to the patent applicants initially for 16 years, which was extendable for 10 more years if the working of the patent had not sufficiently been remunerative to the patentee. This Act did not specifically mention which kind of right, product or process would be granted to the applicants. According to the interpretation of the patent office, both product and process were patentable. But there was a provision in this Act which made the grant of any such right virtually equivalent to grant of product patent. According to this provision the patentee, while patenting a new product, could describe not only all known processes but also all probable processes of producing the patented product in his patent application. The multinational companies (MNCs) exploited this clause in such a manner that enabled them to enjoy a monopoly status for at least 16 years even if they were not categorically granted product patent. It became possible because probable processes were also protected by the right already granted.

Another important feature of this 1911 Act was that the right to importation was also given to the patentee. This was again detrimental to the developmental prospect of the underdeveloped countries. When a country issues monopoly right to an inventor for his product it usually expects that the product will be produced and sold within its national territory. The rationale behind this expectation is that it will then provide some impetus to the developmental prospect of the country by way of providing employment opportunities to some people. Thus, if the right to importation is extended to the patent holder, it will go against the interest of the country, especially if it is an underdeveloped one.

Realizing that a drastic change in our patent law is necessary for building up a strong and effective platform for rapid industrialization, attempts to amend the law were initiated immediately after the independence. Accordingly, a 'Patent Enquiry Committee' was set up in 1950 under the chairmanship of Baxi Tekchand, a retired judge of Lahore High Court. The committee opined in its report that the 1911 Act was neither succeeded in generating any impetus among the Indians for new inventions, nor did it create any initiative for industrial applications of new inventions. Thereafter, several attempts were made for the revision of the 1911 Act. The Parliament too debated over a number of Patent Bills in 1950, 1953, 1965 and 1967. Finally, a new act, The Patent Act 1970, was passed in 1970 which came into effect from 1972.

5.2.1.2. The Patent Act 1970

The Patent Act 1970 had a tremendous impact on Indian economy, especially on manufacturing of drugs and foods. This Act categorically introduced product patent but along with a few exceptions. According to Section 5 of this Act, in case of drugs, foods and products manufactured by chemical processes, patent can be granted only for a new method or process of manufacture, not for the product as a whole. It was not only that mere process patent was permissible under this Act for drugs and foods, but unlike in the previous patent regime, the patentee cannot patent all the processes known to him even if those are new. This section of the Act gave a boost to our indigenous drug manufacturer. Drugs, almost all over the entire world, are usually discovered and patented by the big MNCs. The 1970 Act helped our indigenous firms to manufacture a drug only by developing a new method not mentioned in the patent application of the original drug.

It is therefore clear that the objective of the 1970 Act was to serve the interests of the inventor only after safeguarding the interests of the common people. In order to safeguard public interests, for example, under Section 87 of the Act, every patent relating to food and drug manufacturing process had to be endorsed with the words 'licenses of right' after three years of date of sealing. The words 'licenses of right' imply automatic issuances of licenses by the patentee to anyone willing to use the patent on payment of royalties. Over and above, a provision of granting compulsory license was made in the 1970 Act. The Controller of Patent was empowered to grant, even before the expiry of three years, compulsory license if it is felt necessary in public interest (Section 97).

It is in line with this broad objective that a number of subjects were left outside of 1970 Act. Apart from universal exceptions of inventions contrary to public order, law, morality and inventions injurious to human, animal or plant's life and health, the execution list includes method of agriculture or horticulture, any process for the treatment of human, animals or plants, etc. (Nayar, 1992). All these items, however, are patentable in USA. In fact, in developed countries like USA, almost everything is patentable. This is so because in these countries most of the products are invented in the laboratories of MNCs. Hence declaration of any product to be non-patentable may have serious dampening effect on the profitability of MNCs.

The world trade of pharmaceutical products is generally under the full control of MNCs which had their origin mostly in developed countries. These companies invest huge resources in research projects to develop new drugs. After developing a new drug, these companies demand a protection under the patent law for a considerable period of time so that within the period of protection they can reap a sizeable amount of profit which would be able to over-compensate their entire investment expenditure.

Thus, when India ruled out product patent in drugs in her Patent Act, it came as a serious blow to the drug manufacturing MNCs. On the other hand, taking full advantage of this provision, Indian pharmaceutical companies started producing drugs at a very low cost. In fact, they were not producing any new drugs, rather drugs already discovered and produced by the MNCs were being produced by them with only new process. This practice of Indian companies very soon made them able to capture a major share of home as well as world pharmaceutical market.

This evoked, for obvious reason, adverse reaction among the MNCs, particularly those of American origin. The ultimate outcome of this adverse reaction was the inclusion of the issue of intellectual property protection under the ambit of GATT 1986 agreement. This was done in order to prevent the irresistible advancement of Indian drug industry.

The GATT 1986 accord developed an IPR framework in line with the Paris Convention. Like the Paris Convention, the TRIPS agreement put its main emphasis on the introduction of product patent for any kind of invention. However, unlike the Paris Convention it specified the tenure of the patent right at 20 years. There seems to be no logic behind this magic figure of 20 years, except that the European Community (EC) and the USA have this patent term and Japan, after disagreeing initially with the EC and the USA in the TRIPS negotiations, fell in line (Dhar & Rao, 1992). Moreover, after the termination of product patent, a patentee can opt for process patent also, the term for which is again 20 years. This means that if one can once invent a product, he will be eligible for enjoying a monopoly right over his invention for 40 years in a row. Such a provision clearly goes against the basic objective of patent laws to promote research activities for the benefit of human race because once a product is patented under the new act, none will be interested in developing a better model of that at least for 40 years.

Following the US patent law, the TRIPS agreement also seeks to extend the coverage area of new Patent Acts by the inclusion of life forms like microorganisms, plants, etc. This extension has a serious detrimental effect, particularly on developed economies, because a large section of population there depends on herbal plants for medicine. However, in spite of these limitations and drawbacks, since India was a signatory of GATT 1986 agreement, she was compelled to amend her Patent Act in conformity with TRIPS agreement.

5.2.1.3. Three Amendments

In order to comply with the TRIPS agreement, India was compelled to amend her Patent Act of 1970. The necessary amendments were done in three phases. Accordingly, three new acts, namely, The Patents (Amendment) Act 1999, The Patents (Amendment) Act 2002 and The Patents (Amendment) Act 2005 were enacted.

The first amendment in 1999 was made just to accommodate a few transitional arrangements like filling of product patent application, granting of Exclusive Marketing Rights, etc.

The most important amendments to the 1970 Act were made in the second phase, i.e. in the 2002 Amendment. Some of the important changes that were brought by this Amendment can be summarized as follows:

First of all, Section 3 of the 1970 Act enumerated what are not 'inventions' and those inventions, which are not patentable. This list was modified by The Patents (Amendments) Act 2002. After amendment, an invention that is frivolous or contrary to well-established natural laws cannot be patentable. An invention intended to commercial exploitation or contrary to public order or morality or which causes serious prejudice to human, animal or plant life or health or to the environment, is also not patentable. Mere arrangement, rearrangement or duplication of a known device cannot be patented. Mere discovery of a scientific principle or the formulation of an abstract theory or 'discovery of any living thing or non-living substance occurring in nature' is not acceptable (Raju, 2004).

Secondly, Section 4(j) excludes plants and animals other than micro-organisms in whole or any part thereof including seeds, varieties and species and essentially biological processes for production or propagation of plants and animals.

Thirdly, Section 4(p) excludes an invention, which, in effect, is traditional knowledge or which is an aggregation or duplication of known properties of traditionally known component or components.

Fourthly, the term of protection for all categories of invention as per Article 33 of the TRIPS Agreement has been prescribed to 20 years from the date of filing of patent application.

Fifthly, by the Patent Act the applicant must submit with his/her application a specification of the said invention. By the Section 10(1) of The Patent Act 1970 'every specification, whether provisional or complete, shall describe the invention and shall begin with a title sufficiently indicating the subject-matter to which the invention relates'. The 2002 Amendment specifies that, 'if the applicant mentions a biological material in the specification' he/she must 'disclose the source and geographical origin of the biological material in the specification, when used in an invention'.

After all these amendments practically, nothing was left for the 2005 amendment. The 2005 Amendment extended product patent protection uniformly to all fields of technology including food, chemicals and drugs.

5.2.2 Geographical Indications of Goods (Registration and Protection) Act, 1999

India enacted her Geographical Indications of Goods (Registration and Protection) Act in the year 1999, which came into effect from 2003. Under this Act right holders have to register their GI with the Geographical Indications Registry of the Government of India. The registration will then enable the registered owner to opt for seeking relief against any kind of infringement.

Under the present Act, the GI can be obtained for any agricultural, natural or manufactured goods, which either originated or manufactured in the territory of the country, or a region or locality in that territory. In case of agricultural or natural goods, GI can be claimed, if and only if, a given quality, reputation or other characteristics of such goods is essentially attributable to its geographical origin. In case of the manufactured goods, on the other hand, at least one of production, processing and preparation, of the good must take place in the concerned territory, region or locality for the good to be eligible for obtaining the GI.

Any association of persons or producers or any organization or authority established under any law, who are desirous to protect the interest of the producers of the good intended to be protected can apply for the registration of GI for the good. According to Indian GI Act, any name, even if it is not the name of a country, region or locality of that country, shall also be considered to be a GI if it relates to a specific geographical area and is used upon the concerned good. Owing to this rule, Basmati, a special kind of rice grain produced in the foothill region of the Himalayas, obtained GI registration.

5.2.3 Copyright Act, 1957

The first Copyright Act was enacted in India in 1847, just 100 years ago of India's independence. The Act passed by the Governor General of India practically affirmed the applicability of English copyright law to India. In order to get protection under the Act, registration of the work with the Home Office was mandatory. The term of copyright under the Act was for the lifetime of the author plus seven years, but in no case would it be more than 42 years. Before independence, this Act was amended twice, once in the year 1911 and then in the year 1914.

The independent India enacted her first Copyright Act in the year 1957. This 1957 Act went through various amendments in the years 1983, 1984, 1992, 1994, 1999 and very recently in 2012. The amendments in 1994 and in 1999 were made to accommodate the terms of the TRIPS agreement.

The office of the Registrar of Copyright was established by this Act. This Act extended copyright protection to (1) original literary, dramatic, musical and artistic works; (2) cinematographic films and (3) sound recording.

By this Act, (1) 'literary work' includes computer programmes, tables and compilations including computer [Sec 2(o)]; (2) 'dramatic work' includes any piece for recitation, choreographic work or entertainment in dumb show, the scenic arrangement or acting, form of which is fixed in writing or otherwise but does not include a cinematograph film [Sec 2(h)]; (3) 'musical work' means a work consisting of music and includes any graphical notation of such work but does not include any words or any action intended to be sung, spoken or performed with the music [Sec 2(p)]; (4) 'artistic work' means a painting, a sculpture, a drawing (including a diagram, map, chart or plan), an engraving or a photograph, whether or not any such work possesses artistic quality; a work of architecture;

any other work of artistic craftsmanship [Sec 2(c)]; (5) 'cinematograph film' means any work of visual recording or any medium produced through a process from which a moving image may be produced by any means and includes a sound recording accompanying such visual recording and 'cinematograph' shall be construed as including any work produced by any process analogous to cinematography including video films [Sec 2(f)]; (6) 'sound recording' means a recording of sounds from which such sounds may be produced regardless of the medium on which such recording is made or the method by which the sounds are produced [Sec 2(xx)]. By this Act, the copyright means the exclusive right to do or authorize the doing of some acts like reproducing, making copies, translating, making any adaption, performing, selling, etc. in respect of any work or any substantial part thereof.

The Act offered a protection right which would be effective up to 50 years after the death of the author. The author shall start enjoying this right immediately after its creation. For enjoying this right, no registration shall essentially be required. However, if anyone makes his work registered it will help him in litigations arising out of infringement.

5.2.4 Biodiversity Act, 2002

The most important Act of India which addresses the concern of traditional knowledge holders is the Biological Diversity Act 2002. India enacted this law in accordance with her ratification of the CBD, (1992). The CBD gave recognition to the sovereign rights of the states over their own biological resources. It called for the enactment of national laws by the member countries to exploit this sovereign right.

The objective of the Act, as stated in its Preamble is 'to provide for conservation of biological diversity, sustainable use of its components and fair and equitable sharing of the benefits arising out of the use of biological resources[15], knowledge and for matters connected therewith or incidental thereto'. In the Preamble, the Act acknowledges that 'India is rich in biological diversity and associated traditional and contemporary knowledge system relating thereto'. To safeguard this richness the primary objective of the Act is to prohibit foreign nationals or corporates in obtaining 'any biological resource occurring in India or knowledge associated thereto for research or for commercial utilization or for bio-survey and bio-utilization'. In order to obtain such resources or/and associated knowledge, foreign nationals have to take permission from National Biodiversity Authority (NBA).

The permission mechanism shall be applied for Indian citizens and organization also. They have to take prior approval of State Biodiversity Board. However, no such permission procedure has been made applicable for to the local people and communities of the area, including growers and cultivators of biodiversity, and *vaids* and *hakims*, who have been practicing indigenous medicine [Section 7].

Constitution of the NBA is a major decision towards developing a safeguard mechanism. By Section 3 of this Act, the NBA is empowered to give permission to (1) a person who is not a citizen of India, (2) a citizen of India, but non-resident, to obtain any biological resource occurring in India or knowledge associated thereto for research or for commercial utilization or for bio-survey and bio-utilization. Not only the use of biological resource occurring in India or knowledge associated thereto is restricted, but also the transfer of the results of any research relating to these resources and knowledge to any foreign national, non-resident Indian or any organization which is not registered or incorporated in India or which has any non-Indian participation in its share capital or management is prohibited, without the approval of the NBA, for monetary or other consideration (Section 4). However, publication of research papers or dissemination of such knowledge in any seminar or workshop is permissible if such publication abides by the guidelines issued by the Central Government.

Moreover, any person who wants to apply for any IPR, in or outside India, for any invention based on any research or information on a biological resource obtained from India must take prior approval from the NBA (Section 6.1). The NBA may, while granting the approval, impose benefit sharing fee or royalty or both or impose conditions including the sharing of financial benefits arising out of the commercial utilization of such rights (Section 6.2).

In this regard, Section 21(1) categorically states 'that the terms and conditions subject to which approval is granted secures equitable sharing of benefits arising out of the use of accessed biological resources, their by-products, innovations and practices associated with their use and applications and knowledge relating thereto in accordance with mutually agreed terms and conditions between the person applying for such approval, local bodies concerned and the benefit claimers'[16].

In case of monetary benefits, the NBA may direct the benefits to be paid directly to the benefit claimers or to deposit the same to the National Biodiversity Fund. Section 21(3) states that 'where biological resource or knowledge was a result of access from specific individual or group of individuals or organizations, the National Biodiversity Authority may direct that the amount shall be paid directly to such individual or group of individuals or organizations in accordance with the terms of any agreement and in such manner as it deems fit'. Otherwise the amount should be deposited to the National Biodiversity Fund.

The National Biodiversity Fund constituted by the present Act [Section 27 (1)] should be built upon: (1) any grants and loans made to the National Biodiversity Authority by the Central Government; (2) all charges and royalties received by the National Biodiversity Authority under this Act and (3) all sums received by the National Biodiversity Authority from such other sources as may be decided upon by the Central Government.

The Fund shall be applied for (1) channelling benefits to the benefit claimers; (2) conservation and promotion of biological resources and development of areas from where such biological resources or knowledge associated thereto has been accessed; (3) socio-economic development of areas from where such biological resources or knowledge associated thereto has been accessed in consultation with the local bodies concerned.

The Biological Diversity Act, as we have stated earlier, primarily focuses on developing a protectionist mechanism against bio-piracy. But what would be the role of the Act in case of an event of grant of IPRs in any country outside India on any biological resource obtained from India or knowledge associated with such biological resource which is derived from India? The Act bestows the power on the NBA to oppose any such grant on behalf of the Government of India [Section 18(4)].

5.2.5 Protection of Plant Varieties and Farmer's Rights Act, 2001 (PPVRA, 2001)

Patent is limited in its scope in the sense that this right can be extended only to the inventions which have industrial applications, and which are essentially non-living. There is a reason behind why living objects are made excludable from being patenting. An application for a product to get patented can be submitted only with the submission of a provisional or completed specification of the product. This is not possible for any living object. But the question of giving protection to the living materials started coming very much in the arena of IPR laws after the development of biotechnology in the second half of the twentieth century. Not only the question of protection but also a pressure in this regard came from the multinational companies who were funding the research studies on biotechnology. The result of this pressure came finally in the form of TRIPS agreement. Article 27.3(b) of TRIPS states that,

> *Members may exclude from patentability plants and animals other than micro-organisms, and essentially biological processes for the production of plants or animals other than non-biological and microbiological processes. However, members shall provide for the protection of plant varieties either by patents or by an effective* sui generis *system or by any combination thereof.*

India finally decided to enact a *sui generis* system to protect her plant varieties along with farmer's interest. The Act, Protection of Plant Varieties and Farmer's Rights Act, was passed by the Indian Parliament in the year 2001. The objective of the Act is:

> *...the establishment of an effective system for the protection of the plant varieties, the protection of the rights of the farmers and the breeders, recognition of the contribution farmers in conserving and improving the plant genetic resource, stimulate the investment to promote the research and development in the public and the private sectors so as to make available the quality seeds to the farmers, thereby encouraging the accelerated growth of the agricultural sector and to carry out the obligation arising out of the TRIPS Agreement of WTO.*

For the protection of plant varieties what is required first is the registration of seed varieties. The Act makes provision of registration of two types of seeds namely, the extant variety and farmers' variety. In the Act, the extant variety is defined as a variety available in India which is, (1) notified under Section 5 of the Seeds Act, 1966; or (2) farmer's variety; or (3) a variety about which there is common knowledge or (4) any other variety which is in public domain.

The seeds are to be registered under the Plant Varieties Registry. Both the extant varieties and the farmers' varieties can be registered under the Act only when they are confirming to the criteria of novelty, distinctiveness, uniformity and stability. An application for the registration of a plant variety can be submitted by (1) the breeder of the variety; (2) successor of the breeder of the variety; (3) the assignee of the breeder of the variety; (4) farmers or group of farmers or community of farmers claiming to be the breeder of the variety and (5) any university or publicly funded agricultural institution claiming to be the breeder of the variety.

The registration of a variety confers an exclusive right on the breeder or his successors, his agent or licensee to produce, sell, market, distribute, import or export the variety (Section 28). Let us now, one by one, describe the rights this Act confers on the farmers, breeders and the holders of TK.

1. Rights to the farmers:

   According to PPVRA 2001,a farmer is a person who (1) cultivates crops by cultivating the land himself; or (2) cultivates crops by directly supervising the cultivation of land through any other person; or (3) conserves and preserves, severally or jointly, with any other person any wild species or traditional varieties or adds value to such wild species or traditional varieties through selection and identification of their useful properties.

   Farmer's rights in this Act arise from their role in conserving, improving and making plant genetic resources available for developing newer varieties. Two basic roles of farmers have been recognized by the present Act. First of all, it is acknowledged that farmers traditionally conserve genetic resources of land races and wild varieties of economic plants. Secondly, farmers through selection and use of traditional breeding method can develop new varieties of seeds. Provisions are built in this Act to protect the rights of the farmers for both the roles. The farmers can register the seed they developed. After registration, besides selling, they can, as usual, save, use, sow, re-sow, exchange or share the seed variety protected under the Act. On the other hand, for his role in conserving genetic resources of land races and wild varieties of economic plants, a farmer can get rewarded from the Gene Fund.

The National Gene Fund, according to this Act, is to be constituted by the Central Government. The Fund shall mainly be used for the payment towards benefit sharing and towards the expenditure for supporting the conservation and sustainable use of genetic resources including in situ and ex situ collections.

The concept of benefit sharing is a unique feature of this Act. Introduction of the provision of benefit sharing, in fact, recognizes the role of a typical farmer in conserving the plant genetic materials once again. After granting a certificate of registration to the breeder for the new variety, the Protection and Plant Varieties and Farmers Rights Authority notifies the details of the protected varieties and invites claims for benefit sharing.

2. Rights to the breeders:

   This Act is mainly meant for upholding the breeder's right. Under the Act, a breeder can register his plant variety and can enjoy the rights of a plant breeder. The holder of a plant breeder right enjoys the exclusive right to produce, sell, market and distribute the seeds of the protected variety.

3. Rights to the holders of TK:

   The Act did not specifically mention anything regarding rights of TK holder, but there are some provisions in the Act which can uphold the interest of the TK holders. For example, Section 18.1(e) states that:

> *...every application for registration [...] shall contain a complete passport data of the parental lines from which the variety has been derived along with the geographical location in India from where the genetic material has been taken and all such information relating to the contribution, if any, of any farmer, village community, institution or organisation in breeding, evolving or developing the variety.*

This section, therefore, made the acknowledgement of the contribution of the traditional farmers' community in breeding, evolving or developing certain varieties of seeds mandatory for the applicant. However, the Act did not stop by making this acknowledgement mandatory. In Section 18.1(h), it states that:

> *...every application for registration [...] shall contain a declaration that the genetic material or parental material acquired for breeding, evolving or developing the variety has been lawfully acquired.*

The implication of the use of the word 'lawfully' would be clear if we take into account Section 40 of the Act, which is as follows:

> *A breeder or other person making application for registration of any variety shall disclose in the*

> *application the information regarding the use of genetic material conserved by any tribal or rural families in the breeding or development of such variety.*
>
> Section 40(1).

> *If the breeder or such other person fails to disclose any information under sub-section (1), the Registrar may, after being satisfied that the breeder or such person has willfully and knowingly concealed such information, reject the application for registration.*
>
> Section 40(2).

It may happen that the breeder failed to collect authentic information regarding the contribution of a farmer or of a village community. In that case, decision should be left to the Authority, which can invite claims later through media/public notices etc. (Brahmi, et al., 2004).

5.2.6 The Seeds Bill

In order to extend proper protection to the farmers' rights in the context of new IPR regime after the TRIPS Agreement, the Government of India, in the year 2004, initiated an amendment to her Seeds Act of 1966. The Seeds Bill, introduced in the upper house of the Indian Parliament on December 09, 2004, sought for regulating the markets of seeds and plant materials so as to ensure supply of improved quality of seeds, increase private participation in production and distribution of seeds, and liberalizing imports of seeds, while incorporating measures to protect rights of farmers.

Immediately after introduction, the Bill started facing opposition from various stakeholders, particularly from farmers, who recognized it as a threat on their traditional rights over seeds. The draft of the Seeds Bill 2004, therefore, has been revised three times to accommodate concerns expressed by farmers' bodies, civil society and also the parliamentarians (Singh, 2015). But even after third revision in 2011, the Bill is yet to be passed by the Parliament to make the Seed Act 1966 amended. The salient features of the Bill after third revision may be mentioned as follows: (1) Each variety of seeds is to be registered before sale; (2) To be registered, seeds must meet the prescribed minimum standard; (3) The farmers will be exempted from maintaining the prescribed minimum standard while selling the seeds of their own farm; (4) The farmers can use the seeds of their own farm, but can't sell the same under a brand name; (5) The farmers are entitled to get compensation from the seller of the seed, in case a registered seed used by them fails to meet the expected standards; (6) Disputes regarding compensation will be settled by the Compensation Committee.

The Seeds Bill has gone through a lot of changes since its inception. Several sections which previously were going against the interests of the farmers were made corrected. For example, as per Seeds Bill 2004, the farmer also needs to conform the minimum prescribed standard of their seeds for selling them in the market. Continuous representations from farmers lobby made this clause to be revoked.

It is of no doubt that all these changes made the Bill much more farmer friendly. Besides that, it can't also be denied that some issues are yet to be addressed. For example, making provision of multilateral trade of seeds is praiseworthy, but along with this provision there must also be another profession that can restrict certification from foreign agencies, scientific evidences of similarity in agro-climatic conditions are insured.

However, what is most alarming is that there remain some inconsistencies between the Plant Protection Act and the Seeds

Bill. For example, the Seeds Bill speaks of compulsory registration of seeds, but it does not speak anything about what should happen to the varieties which are already protected under the Plant Protection Act. This will enable the seed producers to get their seeds registered under the Seed Act without mentioning the details of the seed and thereby bypass the benefit sharing with those who have actually developed the varieties. Moreover, the period of registration is not the same under the two Acts. These discrepancies must be rectified. However, it has been learnt from media sources that a final draft is going to propose some more amendments which include a clause to ensure uniformity in laws (Seth, 2017).

5.3 INITIATIVES IN OTHER COUNTRIES

5.3.1 The Philippines

The Philippines enacted her *sui generis* law to protect traditional knowledge, especially TCEs, in 1997. The Act categorically declares that

> *...the State shall recognize, respect and protect the rights of Indigenous Cultural Communities/ Indigenous Peoples (ICCs/IPs) to preserve and develop their cultures, traditions and institutions. It shall consider these rights in the formulation of national laws and policies.*
>
> [Section 2(c)].

Section 34 of this Act states that:

> *ICCs/IPs are entitled to the recognition of the full ownership and control and protection of their*

> *cultural and intellectual rights. They shall have the right to special measures to control, develop and protect their sciences, technologies and cultural manifestations, including human and other genetic resources, seeds, including derivatives of these resources, traditional medicines and health practices, vital medicinal plants, animals and minerals, indigenous knowledge systems and practices, knowledge of the properties of flora and fauna, oral traditions, literature, designs and visual and performing arts.*

The Act, in Section 3(o), also defines that the term:

> *Indigenous Cultural Communities/Indigenous Peoples refer to a group of people or homogenous societies identified by self-ascription and ascription by others, who have continuously lived as organized community on communally bounded and defined territory, and who have, under claims of ownership since time immemorial, occupied, possessed and utilized such territories, sharing common bonds of language, customs, traditions and other distinctive cultural traits, or who have, through resistance to political, social and cultural inroads of colonization, non-indigenous religions and cultures, became historically differentiated from the majority of Filipinos.*

What is most important in developing a *sui generis* law to protect TK is the recognition of community-based knowledge and the rights of the holders of this knowledge. This recognition was extended by Section 32. Section 32 states that:

> *ICCs/IPs have the right to practice and revitalize their own cultural traditions and customs. The State*

> *shall presence, protect and develop the past, present and future manifestations of their cultures as well as the right to the restitution of cultural, intellectual religious, and spiritual property taken without their free and prior informed consent or in violation of their laws, traditions and customs.*

Another important issue in safeguarding the interests of the holders of traditional knowledge is the issue of right to access this knowledge and sharing the accrued benefits there from. Regarding this issue, Section 35 of the present Act states that,

> *...access to biological and genetic resources and to indigenous knowledge related to the conservation, utilization and enhancement of these resources, shall be allowed within ancestral lands and domains of the ICCs/IPs only with a free and prior informed consent of such communities, obtained in accordance with customary laws of the concerned community.*

5.3.2 Panama

Another important act in protecting the rights of the holders of the traditional knowledge is the Panama Act 20 of 2000. The nomenclature of the Act is Special System for the Collective Intellectual Property Rights of Indigenous Peoples. Article 1 of the Act specifies the purpose of the Act which is:

> *...to protect the collective intellectual property rights and traditional knowledge of indigenous peoples in their creations, such as inventions, models, drawings and designs, innovations contained in the images, figures, symbols, graphics, stone carvings and other details; as well as the cultural elements of their*

> *history, music, art and traditional forms of artistic expression suitable for commercial use, via a special system to register, promote and market their rights, in order to highlight the social and cultural values of indigenous cultures and guarantee social justice for them.*

By Article 4:

> *...this Act recognizes the collective rights of indigenous peoples in their musical instruments, music, dances or performances, the oral and written expressions that are part of their traditions and make up their historical, cosmological and cultural expression.*

However, to enjoy this right the knowledge-holders must register their collective rights with the:

> *...respective Congresses or traditional indigenous authorities to the Directorate General of Registration of Industrial Property of the Ministry of Commerce and Industry or to the National Copyright Directorate of the Ministry of Education, as appropriate, for approval and registration. The collective rights of indigenous peoples, once registered, shall neither lapse nor have a fixed duration.*
>
> (Article 7)

Anyone, other than the concerned communities can commercially use the registered knowledge, however, with prior consent. Article 20 of the Act, on this point, states:

> *The industrial reproduction, in whole or in part, of traditional dress and other collective rights recognized in this Act is hereby prohibited, unless*

> *authorized by the Ministry of Commerce and Industry, with the prior express consent of indigenous general congresses and councils, and as long as it does not contravene the provisions of this Act.*

5.4.1 Africa

The African Model Law for the Protection of the Rights of Local Communities, Farmers, Breeders and Regulation of Access to Biological Resources (African Model Law) was enacted in 2000. The Law, first of all, gives due recognition to the sovereign rights of the State and people over their biological resources and confers on them the duty to regulate access to biological resources and to community knowledge and technologies. The Law also acknowledges the need to promote and support traditional and indigenous technologies for in the conservation and sustainable use of biological resources and to complement them by appropriately developed modern technologies. However, in regard to patenting of life forms the Law expresses its view that

> *...all forms of life are the basis for human survival, and, therefore, the patenting of life, or the exclusive appropriation of any life form or part or derivative thereof violates the fundamental human right to life.*

The main aim of this legislation shall be to ensure the conservation, evaluation and sustainable use of biological resources, including agricultural genetic resources, and knowledge and technologies in order to maintain and improve their diversity as a means of sustaining all life support systems (Part I). In this regard, some specific objectives are also mentioned. Important among them are to (1) provide an appropriate system of access to biological resources, community knowledge and technologies subject to the prior informed consent of the State and the concerned local communities; (2) promote appropriate mechanisms for a fair and equitable sharing of benefits arising from the use of biological resources, knowledge and technologies; (3) ensure the effective participation of concerned communities, with a particular focus on women, in making decisions as regards the distribution of benefits which may derive from the use of their biological resources, knowledge and technologies; (4) provide appropriate institutional mechanisms for the effective implementation and enforcement of the rights of local communities, including farming communities and breeders, and the conditions of access to biological resources, community knowledge and technologies.

This legislation applies to biological resources, the derivatives of the biological resources and community knowledge and technologies without affecting (1) the traditional systems of access, use or exchange of biological resources; (2) access, use and exchange of knowledge and technologies by and between local communities. This aspect of the Law is particularly important because the basic objective of the MNCs of the developed world is to destroy this traditional system of farming in order to smooth sailing of their seed business. Once the system of exchanging biological matters and the knowledge regarding their use is prohibited, the passage for selling seeds which can be used only once will be opened up before the MNCs. This will certainly destroy the backbone of the agricultural system of the poor, underdeveloped countries and compel them to succumb to the monopoly power of seed giants. The economic impact of this clause of the Law is, therefore, beyond debate.

In Part IV, the rights of communities over their biological resources and their innovations, practices, knowledge and technologies acquired through generations are recognized. This recognition gives birth to the requirement of permission to access biological resources, innovations, practices, knowledge and technologies regarding their uses by anyone who is not the member of the concerned communities. The granting of an access permit shall be carried out by the National Competent Authority[17] or any person duly authorized to do so (Part 3.7.1). The access permit shall only be valid if there is a written prior informed consent of the concerned community or communities.

The Law also imposes conditions of benefit sharing on granting access permit. Part 3.12 states that:

1. The access permit should be subject to the payment, made before commencement of collection, of a fee the sum of which will depend on whether or not the collection is to be used for commercial purposes, and the number of samples, the area of collecting, the duration of collection and whether or not the collector is granted exclusive rights.

2. The State and the community or communities shall be entitled to a share of the earning derived from when any biological resource and/or knowledge collected generates, directly or indirectly, a product used in a production process.

The local communities, however, have the right to refuse access to their biological resources, innovations, practices, knowledge and technologies where such access will be detrimental to the integrity of their natural or cultural heritage (Part 4.19).

6

HOW FIT ARE THE EXISTING INTELLECTUAL PROPERTY RIGHTS LAWS IN PROTECTING TRADITIONAL KNOWLEDGE?

6.1 INTRODUCTION

The demand for protecting traditional knowledge (TK) arose out of the fact that this knowledge base of aboriginal communities is being continuously misappropriated by the private enterprises, especially multinational companies, all over the world. The worst sufferers are the developing countries, who are coincidentally the owners of these knowledge stores.

There has been extensive discussion within the international community as to the nature of protection that is to be given for traditional knowledge. Solutions have been proposed in the form of defensive protection and positive protection. Defensive protection refers to provisions adopted in law or by the regulatory authorities to prevent intellectual property rights (IPRs) claims relating to TK or a cultural expression or a product being granted to unauthorized persons. Positive protection on the other hand refers to the acquisition of IPRs by the TK holders themselves or an alternative regulatory mechanism under a *sui generis* system.

However, the existing legal structure on IPRs, as it has been seen, is inadequate to prevent the misappropriation of TK. An assessment to evaluate some of the problems and gaps in the present IPR legislations is, therefore, very essential. But before entering into any such analysis, some common limitations due to which it is difficult to use the existing IPR laws in protecting TK may be mentioned. They are as follows: (1) traditional knowledge is often held collectively by communities, rather than by individual owners; (2) communities' concerns about traditional knowledge typically span generations, a much longer timeframe[1] than the duration of most IPRs laws provide; (3) the cost of reliance on the IPRs laws is very high.

6.2 LIMITATIONS OF PATENT

By the Patent Act of India, 1970 only inventions, not discoveries, are patentable. Discovery means unveiling of something, product or process, for the first time which is already in existence. For example, turmeric is a natural product. The healing property of turmeric was once discovered, not invented, by someone. Invention, on the other hand, is the outcome of one's intellect and industry. Generally we distinguish between discovery and invention in this way. In the language of the aforesaid Act 'the mere discovery of any new property or new use for a known substance or process' is not invention and hence beyond patentability. The Patent (amendment) Act, 2005 defines 'invention' in a new way. By this amendment, invention means any new product or process the subject matter of which has not fallen in the public domain or does not form part of the state of the art prior to the date of filing of patent application with complete specification.

If we now note this definition of invention carefully it would be clear to us that the TK cannot be patented. First of all, the TK is 'mere discovery of any new property or new use for a known substance or process'. Secondly, being community knowledge, this knowledge always lies in public domain, although the size of the domain is very small. Since most of the TK lies for a long period in the public domain, it would be difficult to satisfy the novelty and/or inventive step criterion in order to get patent protection (Nunez, 2007).

Moreover, Patent Act, all over the world, is extendable to the products which have industrial applicability. Traditional knowledge may, in some cases, be eligible for industrial application. For example, traditional knowledge regarding medicine can well be applicable for industrial production. But traditional cultural expressions do not allow for industrial application.

Finally, after several amendments, The Patent Act 1970 of India categorically excludes inventions which are effectively in TK from patentability. In Section 3, the Act enlisted some inventions which are not inventions within the meaning of the Act This list of inventions includes 'an invention which, in effect, is traditional knowledge or which is an aggregation or duplication of known properties of traditionally known component or components'.

6.3 LIMITATIONS OF PLANT PATENT

The Patent Act is not applicable to living organisms. But the advent of biotechnology, especially after 1960s, raised the demand for protection of products derived essentially from bio-resources. Article 27.3(b) of the TRIPS agreement has made provision for the member countries of the WTO to introduce *sui generis* law or to make amendments in the existing patent laws for the protection of plant varieties. Accordingly, countries like India enacted their own *sui generis* laws. However, these plant patent laws also have some limitations in protecting the interest of the traditional knowledge holders.

First of all, plant patent laws can protect plant varieties discovered or developed by the farmers or the breeders. But the TK relating to plant and plant materials are important not due to the new varieties of plants, rather due to the knowledge of the aboriginal communities regarding the use of the plants or parts thereof either as medicinal or as food article. There is no scope of protecting this intangible, valuable knowledge of the indigenous communities in the plant patent laws.

Secondly, there is a lack of a clear understanding or consistent approach to what is considered a new plant variety. Many indigenous communities have cultivated and maintained plant varieties over many generations (Hansen & VanFleet, 2003). Probably these varieties do not get protection on the ground of lack of novelty. But many plant varieties, which are developed by the breeders and are simply a slight modification to existing types of plants that were developed (cultivated) by indigenous communities, will get registration under the plant patent law.

Thirdly, registration of new varieties of plants under the plant patent laws is costly and cumbersome. It would be very difficult for any traditional community to go through all the registration process.

6.4 LIMITATIONS OF COPYRIGHT ACT

Traditional Cultural Expression (TCE) is a subset of TK. There are two general approaches among States to the legal protection of TCEs. Some believe that TCEs are adequately protected by existing IP systems and that no additional measures or systems of protection are necessary or would be appropriate. Others believe that the establishment of new, specific measures and/or statutory systems is necessary either to complement existing IP rights or act as a substitute for them because they are regarded as inadequate and/or inappropriate (WIPO, 2003).

- Originality

  One of the main, internationally accepted criteria for the protection of copyright of any work is the originality of the work. The criterion of originality is not specifically claimed as a condition of protection under the Berne Convention. However, it is apparent from Article 2.1 that protected works must be intellectual creations and this is reinforced by the use of these words in Article 2.5. The notion of 'originality' is probably the derivation of these two articles. According to both the civil law and the common law legal systems, it seems that a work is 'original' if there is some degree of intellectual effort involved and has not been copied. Like WIPO, the majority of national copyright legislations do not categorically define the meaning of originality. Instead the interpretation of what is to be original has been left mainly to the courts (Nordell, 1957).

  The prerequisite of originality for obtaining copyright may, however, impede the protection of TCEs. In the common law jurisdictions, at least, a relatively low level of creativity is required in order to meet the originality requirement. As a result, it would be much easier for contemporary tradition-based TCEs to get copyright protection provided that some new expression, beyond merely reproducing the traditional form of expression, is added. However, this much may not go against the interest of the aboriginal communities. But what would happen if the new author is an outsider? According to the copyright law the originality requirement could even be met by an author of a contemporary expression of folklore who is not a member of the relevant cultural community in which the tradition originated. This may certainly deny the interest of the concerned community.

- Authorship
  The next problem that would have to be certainly faced in protecting TCEs with the Copyright Act is the identifiable author requirement of the Act. The Copyright Act extends 'authorship' even to multiple authors for a single work, but it does not recognize unknown authors. But the problem with TCEs is that in most of the cases, especially in case of age-old folklores, it would be very difficult to find out the true identity of the author/authors. However, although specific identity of the author/authors is difficult to find out for a particular TCE, it would not be absolutely impossible to identify the originating community or region that particular TCE comes from. Some distinct particularities of an art form or the material used in the making of a folk item can recognize a certain people, community or region wherefrom the said art form or the item is derived. Thus even if an individual creator can't be identified, it is perfectly possible to identify a group of people who is the actual author of a particular form of TCE. Therefore, in order to address the 'authorless' nature of some works, Article 15(4) of the Berne Convention stipulates that countries may legislate to designate a competent authority to represent unknown authors in the case of 'unpublished works where the identity of the author is unknown, but where there is every ground to

presume that he is a national of a country of the Union'. (Torsen & Anderson, 2010).

- Expression, not style
  The third problem will arise in regard to the nature of the TCE for which the protection is sought for under the copyright laws. Generally, copyright protection does not extend to functional aspects, formulaic or other non-original elements of works, such as colours, and techniques used to create a work, or what is sometimes referred to as a work's 'style'. Instead of 'style of a work' this law protects only 'expression of ideas'. By the term 'expression of ideas', the law wants to indicate the ideas which are materialized in some form or the other. But artistic styles associated with TCEs are sometimes be culturally sensitive for the concerned community and hence should not be copied without prior permission. The present structure of copyright law does not provide for any such mechanism of prior permission. Moreover, until and unless a board, or a trust or a society or something like that is formed a-prior beforehand, it would be difficult to obtain such permission. The question will then arise, will be the authority to grant such permission.

- Fixation requirement
  One of the criterions of a work to be protected under the Copyright Act is the tangibility of the work. This is alternatively referred to as the fixation requirement. Article 2.2 of Berne Convention reads:

> *It shall, however, be a matter for legislation in the countries of the Union to prescribe that works in general or any specified categories of works shall not be protected unless they have been fixed in some material form.*

Imposition of this requirement, however, is optional to member countries of the Berne Union. Mentioning of this criterion is even absent in the TRIPS agreement and also in WIPO Copyright Treaty. Owing to this optionality, while some countries make provision for this criterion in their law, some are not. Many national laws, particularly those of common law countries, do require fixation, because this may facilitate establishing the existence of the work and provide a clear and definite basis for rights. Conversely, many countries, in particular countries with a civil law tradition, in Africa, Latin America (Brazil) and Europe (including Belgium, Spain, France, Switzerland, Italy and Germany) do not require fixation. These countries accord protection to a work as soon as it is in a form in which others can perceive it (WIPO, opcit*).*

- Adaptation
  Another threatening challenge faced by the TCEs is the adaptive works. Adaptive works are based upon one or several pre-existing work(s) or upon material from the public domain. They include any form in which a work may be recast, transformed or adapted. These derivative works qualify for copyright protection under present copyright laws if sufficiently original. The copyright laws allow these iterations because, in principle, it supports the derivation of new art forms inspired by pre-existing TCEs. But it does not support unlawful copying or unauthorized adaptation. So, the only solution is to give recognition to each iteration. However, recognizing each new iteration of TCE as derivative work would, first of all, go against the interest of the aboriginal community who originally holds the right and, secondly, would allow each iteration to eventually fall into the public domain and thus be available for further use by anyone.

- Limited term of protection
  Copyright Acts, all over the world, make no provision for indefinite term of protection. After the expiry of the limited term, the protected works ultimately enter the public domain. Both the Berne Convention and the TRIPS agreement stipulate a minimum term of protection which covers the entire life of the author and 50 more years after the death of the author. Presently Indian Copyright Act extends the protection up to 60 years after the death of the author. The longest duration in this regard is provided by Mexico. According to Mexican Copyright Act, copyright lasts for the life of an author plus 75–100 years, dependent upon an array of factors.

  The problem with this provision can be found in the nature of the TCEs. The TCEs are, by nature, intergenerational. It is, therefore, argued that no finite term would be appropriate for their protection. However, extending indefinite protection is no novel concept. For example, royalty rights from use of the famous work 'Peter Pan' subsist in perpetuity under the United Kingdom copyright law for the benefit of a charitable cause (Torsen & Anderson, 2010). Moreover, The Model Provisions 1982 do not ask for any limited term. Similar is the case for the Model law of the Pacific Island countries[18]. Thus building up of a *sui generis* model law for protecting TK can easily overcome this drawback of existing Copyright Act.

6.5 LIMITATIONS OF GEOGRAPHICAL INDICATION ACT

Sometimes, in some countries, Geographical Indications Acts are being used to protect traditional knowledge. Darjeeling Tea in our country may be a classic example of this endeavor. In fact, in some respect the GI Acts have definite advantage over other IPRs Acts, like Patent and Copyright Act, in protecting the interests of the traditional knowledge holders.

First of all, while Patent and Copyright Acts extend individual right, geographical indications are based on the concept of collective rights (Pant, 2015). Geographical indications are outcome of collective enterprise and collective decision making process of a particular community based on a particular region. Hence geographical indications eventually become identifiable with the culture of a particular community of a particular region. Since traditional knowledge is also defined to be a part of the culture of a particular community, GI protection may be a good fit.

Secondly, Patent and Copyright Acts offer protection rights to innovations and creations. Geographical Indication Acts, on the other hand, are designed to reward high standard of quality of 'goods' cultivated over generation after generation to earn goodwill and reputation. Thus a concept of 'tradition' is inherent in geographical indication. In this sense, GI Acts are, once again, good fit for protecting traditional knowledge.

Thirdly, traditional knowledge is necessitated to be protected for indefinite period because it is intergenerational in nature. Both the Patent and Copyright Acts offer protection for limited term. But in GI Act, there is a scope for long-term protection (WIPO, 2017). For example, the Indian GI Act, on this issue, makes provision for an initial registration for a period of 10[19] years (Sec 18.1). Thereafter, the registration may be renewed for a period of 10 years from the date of expiration of the original registration or of the last renewal[20] of registration (Sec. 18.2). Combining these two sections together, it would not be difficult to claim for an indefinite term of protection under the GI Act.

However, in spite of all these advantages, the GI Act may not be ideal for the protection of traditional knowledge. Following are the points that go against the GI Act. First of all, geographical indication is meant to protect only a 'good'. This would exclude all intangible forms of traditional knowledge.

Secondly, geographical indication protection is of assistance only where the knowledge is associated with a defined geographical area. Thus, if the knowledge is scattered as in the case of the Ayurvedic system of medicine a geographical indication cannot be used[21].

6.6 LIMITATIONS OF TRADEMARK

Trademark has definitely certain advantages in protecting indigenous knowledge. First of all, trademark speaks of both individual and collective rights. Hence, traditional knowledge, which often collectively held by communities, rather than by individual owners, can well be protected by the Trademark Act (CIPR, 2002).

Secondly, Trademark Act does not distinguish between tangible and intangible assets. Hence, intangible intellectual properties, like traditional cultural expressions, which can't be protected by Geographical Indications Acts, can get protection under the Trademark Act.

Thirdly, traditional knowledge flows over generations. It, therefore, demands a much longer duration of protection than any other intellectual property. Since trademark allows for unlimited protection with repeated renewal options, it may be a good fit for protecting TK.

But in spite of these advantages, trademark is considered to be the weakest form of IPR laws in protecting TK because trademark can uphold only the commercial interest, if any, of local and indigenous communities. But sometimes, as we have argued earlier, traditional knowledge is more important for its heritage value than that of commercial value. For example, mask dance of Bankura has become, over time, the cultural symbol of local communities of the region. Now if someone from elsewhere apes the dance and does the public performance of the same, it will certainly hurt the cultural sentiment of the concerned community. Trademark can no way prevent such non-commercial use of traditional cultural expressions. But traditional communities, for their communal identity, always prefer protection of both commercial and non-commercial use of their knowledge, which trademarks are unable to extend.

6.7 LIMITATIONS OF TRADE SECRETS

Trade secrets may be the most suitable property right weapon for the holders of traditional knowledge. It has certain advantages over other kinds of IPR laws. For example, unlike patent law trade secrets do not ask for the satisfaction of different criteria like 'novelty', 'non-obviousness' or 'applicability in industrial process'. What it simply requires is the 'secrecy' of the information like the process or the technique or the method (Long, 2012). In fact, if the process of 'reverse engineering' is not applicable to the information, trade secret protection is more preferable than patent protection. However, trade secrets are more suitable for non-medicinal knowledge. Traditional medicinal knowledge, it has been seen that, sometimes loses their secrecy for being used in the public domain for a pretty long time. Owing to the loss of secrecy trade secrets cannot be used in such cases.

Secondly, in case of trade secrets no registration or something like that is required. In view of the holders of traditional knowledge this is important because these people are not familiar with any such formalities.

Thirdly, property right of trade secrets can be enjoyed for an indefinite period if the 'secrecy' can be maintained (Varadarajan, 2011).

The disadvantages of trade secrets in protecting the TK holder's rights can now be listed. First of all, in case of misappropriation of trade secrets, the bearer of the secrets has to sue cases at the court against the unauthorized user. But since there is no separate law for trade secrets, the legal battle has to be fought under the law of confidence. Compensation may be claimed for 'breach of confidence and other acts contrary to honest commercial practices'. The entire process is costly and time-consuming. Moreover, it is cumbersome for the holders of traditional knowledge to go through the hazards of litigation procedure.

Secondly, the bearers of trade secrets will lose their right over the secrets once the secrets are diffused to the public domain (Ogwezzy, 2012). This risk, however, always remains with the traditional knowledge because of their prolonged use. For example, the healing properties of turmeric or insecticidal properties of neem were the discovery of aboriginal communities. But they could be patented by American companies because knowing to these properties of neem and turmeric, the said companies were able to develop new, industrially applicable product of neem and turmeric by their own. These patents can be revoked by the government of India because they were protected under patent regime. Trade secrets will be of no help in such cases. However, it is also true that benefits of trade secrets can be perpetual if licensed properly. In the 1880s, a US citizen, J.J. Lawrence, developed an oral antiseptic, named 'Listerine'. The 'secret formula' was subsequently shared by him with a pharmaceutical company, Warner-Lambert, in lieu of royalty payment to him and to his heirs after his death. Later on the secret formula was published by an American journal. But in the 1950s, a US court ruled that even though the trade secret was now in the public domain, Warner-Lambert had to continue to pay royalties to the J.J. Lawrence heirs as called for under the licensing agreement (Hansen et. al, 2003). Therefore, trade secrets can be applied to traditional knowledge only when there is reasonable effort to maintain the secrecy of the knowledge on the part of the community to which this knowledge belongs to. If no such effort is there, then trade secret protection is not applicable to the traditional knowledge.

7

TOWARDS A NEW LAW

7.1 INTRODUCTION

The issue of traditional knowledge (TK), the role of the holders of the TK in providing important leads to the advancement of Science and Technology, the need to protect the rights of the holders of the TK have previously been discussed in several occasions and also well documented. A few researches have also been done in this field. But the problem of all these studies is that none of them consider different dimensions of TK in a comprehensive manner.

In fact, as we have analyzed before, TK has several dimensions. But there is no single IPR law which can encompass all these dimensions in their framework. For example, Patent Act can't address non-living things, Copyright Act is applicable only to traditional cultural expressions. Again some products can be protected by more than one act. For example, Darjeeling tea in India is now being protected under the Geographical Indications Act. But this product can be protected under the Patent Act as well since tea production goes through some industrial processes. Now it may well happen that two Acts give protection in two different ways which are contradictory in nature.

In India, for example, the issue of protection to seeds has been discussed at least in three occasions namely in Biodiversity Act, in Protection to Plant Varieties and Farmer's Rights Act (PPVRA) and in proposed Seed Bill. And the PPVRA and the Seed Bill have addressed the issue in two opposing ways. The PPVRA was passed in tune with the spirit of the CBD which emphasizes on the protection of farmers' rights. But after the introduction of this Act, the developed countries started putting their pressure on India to introduce another act which can protect the plant breeders' right instead of the farmers'. Accordingly, India initiated a new bill, entitled Seed Bill in 2004 which emphasized on upholding plant breeders' right, bypassing the traditional rights of the farmers.

Under these circumstances, the present study has analyzed different dimensions of TK in a comprehensive manner and suggested for a new law which can encompass different dimensions of TK in a single legal framework. The major dimensions of TK include knowledge on traditional medicine, knowledge on biodiversity, knowledge on agricultural technique and knowledge on traditional cultural expressions. Since each of these dimensions has different character, the present study, for the enactment of a comprehensive law, emphasized on the common characteristics of these different dimensions. For example, each form of TK is community knowledge, each of them are age old, transgenerational and most of them are held in oral or non-codified form. So the new law needs to be framed in such a way that it can protect community knowledge, arrange for longer duration of protection than existing IPR laws, make arrangement for collection and preservation of non-codified knowledge. For the protection of community knowledge, what is essential first is the development of some kind of trust body which will receive the commercial benefit of using TK for commercial purposes. TK is held in both tangible and intangible form. So arrangements must be ready for the collection and preservation of both these forms of knowledge. Among tangible forms of knowledge, we can get living and non-living things. It is quite difficult to preserve living specifications of inventions. For example, it may be impossible for IPR authorities to preserve genetic resources for a long period of time. To resolve this problem, the study suggests developing a Gene Bank where inventor can submit their specifications and it can be preserved as national asset. On the other hand, for the preservation of natural cultural expressions, a Natural Heritage Museum can be built which may also be used for commercial purposes by the government. In a nutshell, it should be remembered that TK are national assets, and their specifications should not be collected for mere granting protection right. One of the reasons that once upon a time patent right did not allow for living objects was because of this specification submission. In a similar manner, oral submission is not difficult to preserve in this age of digital world.

The existing IPR laws make provisions for limited period of production because their intention is to protect individual right. But once community right will be granted, it is not difficult to permit indefinite period of protection. We, therefore, suggest extension of period of protection for communal knowledge. However, it can be allowed only after the suspension of granting protection to TK under the purview of existing IPR laws which upheld private rights only.

The uniqueness and special contribution of the present study lie in these recommendations. The spirit of these recommendations has to be understood with a non-capitalist mindset. The existing IPR laws have been developed and amended under a capitalist framework, which always tries to uphold individual rights. But once we emphasize on upholding communal right, we have to suspend the present structure. It is a totally worthless attempt to accommodate rights of the TK holders under the ambit of existing IPS structure. What I have tried to suggest, therefore, in my study is to develop a totally new framework that can address the issues of communal rights, like the rights of TK holders. None of my predecessors in this field of research has viewed the problem from this angle.

7.2 THE MODEL LAW

The Article 27.3(b) of the TRIPS agreement has made provision for the enactment of *sui generis* law by member countries to protect their plant and animal varieties. Protection of plant varieties is somewhat meaningless if associated TK can't be protected. The WTO gave recognition to this fact in Doha Declaration. Accordingly, a few countries have already enacted their own *sui generis* laws to protect both their bio-resources and associated TK. To name some of the countries included in this list are Peru, Panama, Brazil, Philippines, etc. But no initiatives have yet been seen on behalf of the Government of India to enact any such law.

The first such initiative in India was, however, taken by the National Law School of India University (NLSIU), Bangalore. The TK (Protection and Regulation to Access) Bill 2009 drafted by NLSIU was the first ever attempt in India, for a separate and complete regime for the protection of TK in India. The Bill aims at to provide for protection, conservation and effective management of TK. It emphasizes the need for sustainability of resources on which TK is based as well as ensures the continuation of the customary practices of the TK (Das, 2011). In a nutshell, the main theme of the Bill was the prevention of unauthorized use of TK and vis-a-vis developing an appropriate access and benefit sharing mechanism in case of commercial use of TK by the third parties.

Another attempt was made by Shashi Tharoor, an MP of Indian National Congress from Kerala, to move a private member's bill to provide for the protection, preservation, promotion and development of India's TK. If TK remains in the domains of individuals, communities or trusts, it runs the risk of exploitation by commercial interests and hence it should be with the state. That is the argument put forward by those who want such a bill (Deccan Chronicle, March 9, 2017).

These attempts, in addition to our discussion so far, prove the demand of the hour regarding the introduction of a *sui generis* law to protect our TK, resources, especially bio-resources, required for the use of this knowledge and also the rights of the holders of this knowledge. In enacting such a law, the government must keep the following points in mind:

1. A single law has to be formulated with various subsections to incorporate different dimensions of TK.

2. Presently, issues relating to protection of TK are addressed in various laws like Patent Act, Biological Diversity Act, Farmers' Rights Act, etc. Often they are overlapping and even contradictory in some cases. These overlapping and contradictory issues must have to be identified first. After identifying these sections or sub-sections, they have to be deleted from the concerned law and be incorporated thereafter in the new law. Developing a *sui generis* regime of law for the protection of the TK, therefore, implies, on the one hand, the enactment of a new law and, on the other, rectification of the existing laws. In the new regime of IPR laws, domain of each law should be clearly mentioned.

3. Besides restructuring our IPR laws, an effort should have to continue in the international front to bring harmonization of IPR laws of different countries. This is essential to put an end to bio-piracy. In fact, bio-piracy is an international issue.

Without simultaneous, harmonized effort on the part of various countries, this practice cannot be stopped altogether.

4. The new law should be composed in such a way that it should be easily understandable, accessible and affordable to the poor, mostly illiterate members of communities holding TK.

On the basis of this list of considerations, the objectives of the new law should be:

1. To respect, preserve and ensure judicious use of TK;
2. To encourage the use of TK for research and commercial purpose so that the benefits of such knowledge no longer remain confined to a small community and instead be disseminated over to the entire human race;
3. To encourage the holders of TK by way of monetary and non-monetary benefit to make them engaged in continuous effort for the further advancement of their knowledge;
4. To encourage indigenous communities to conserve local biodiversity so that the future prospect of discovery of yet-to-be-discovered species useful to humankind is not closed for ever;
5. To ensure that TK be used by the outsiders with due acknowledgment to the respective holders of such knowledge;
6. To ensure that the benefits arising out of commercial use of TK be shared fairly and equitably between the users and holders of such knowledge.

Extending protection to the rights of the holders of TK is a two-step process. Firstly, the knowledge is to be registered by the owners of the TK with an appropriate national authority. Secondly, consent for accessing the knowledge from its owners has to be acquired by the prospective user with mutually agreed terms. For the completion of the first step the new law should:

1. Ensure building up of a national authority by the government of respective countries to register knowledge;
2. Make provisions for submitting the document of the specific knowledge the right holders wish to protect. Since TK is held, in most of the cases, in non-codified form, it may not always be possible to submit written documents of the knowledge. The national registration authority should develop the ways and means of documenting this non-codified knowledge. For example, oral submissions can be preserved in digital form. In case of living specifications, like genetic resources, a National Gene Bank may be established. For submission of specifications of traditional cultural expressions, a National Heritage Museum can be established, which can be used by the government for commercial purposes also.
3. Constitute a welfare society or a trust or something like that which will be entrusted with receiving monetary benefits arising out of the commercial use of the knowledge and distributing the same to the stakeholders of TK.
4. Make provisions for a longer period of protection. Since communal rights do not hamper the interests of others, protection for an indefinite period may also be considered.

In completing the first step, one problem may arise due to a special character of the TK. The TK is often community knowledge. The community which possesses the knowledge often be reluctant to disclose them to anyone outside their community. Out of this reluctance, they never encrypt their knowledge anywhere in black and white. Owing to this nature of the TK, the owners of this knowledge may also express their reluctance in documenting the same for even the purpose of protection. Considering how invaluable this knowledge in the registration process may be relaxed to some extent. For example, in registering a product for patent protection, complete disclosure of the invention is a must. In case of registering a TK, some kind of flexibility may be introduced. The owners of such knowledge may be allowed to disclose only the description of the end product in details, instead of disclosing the detailing of the process of derivation.

The second step of the process of extending the protection to the rights of the TK holders is much more crucial. In this regard, the law should make provision for:

1. Guaranteeing that access to any TK be possible only with the prior informed consent of the holders of the TK;
2. Guaranteeing that the owners have the right to grant or deny permission of accessing their knowledge;
3. Guaranteeing that the permission to use the TK commercially be granted only after reaching mutually agreed arrangements for benefit sharing;
4. Ensuring that access right to databases that contain TK be granted only after the payment of access fee. The Government of India has already developed a huge digital database of TK in the name of TKDL. Initiatives of documenting TK have also taken up by several NGOs like Gene Campaign. Biodiversity Boards of different states also started building Biodiversity Registers. All these databases are to be made accessible with access fee. The fund collected in this way should ensure to be shared with the concerned community.

5. Imposing monetary penalty along with punishment of imprisonment for the unauthorized access to the TK. This is vital because the entire initiative of protecting TK has arisen out of regular, continuous and recurring misappropriation of TK. Bio-piracy and misappropriation of associated TK, therefore, should be declared cognizable offense.

6. Building up of a fund to be held commonly by the State and by the community who is the actual owner of the knowledge. The monetary benefits be first deposited by the user to this fund, which is later on be shared among stakeholders, i.e. the State and the concerned communities who possess the rights of the knowledge.

NOTES

1. By recombinant DNA technology, genetic materials of two different organisms are combined together to obtain a new organism with desired characteristics. By this technology, DNA fragments from a variety of sources are inserted into a particular gene via appropriate vector to have a desirable gene sequence.
2. Traditional medicine that has been adopted by other populations (outside its indigenous culture) is often termed 'complementary and alternative medicine' (CAM) (WHO, 2002).
3. According to the definition provided by the CBD 'Biological diversity means the variability among living organisms from all sources including, inter alia, terrestrial, marine and other aquatic ecosystems and the ecological complexes of which they are part; this includes diversity within species, between species and of ecosystems' (Article 2, Para 1: Use of Terms).
4. 'Biological resources' according to the definition provided by the CBD, 'include genetic resources, organisms or parts thereof, populations, or any other biotic component of ecosystems with actual or potential use or value for humanity' (Article 2, Para 2: Use of Terms).

5. Two words 'indigenous people' and 'local community' do not bear similar meaning. Those who voluntarily isolate themselves from the main stream and have distinct linguistic and cultural identity are called indigenous people. Local community, on the other hand, may mix with the main stream of population but they possess a little bit knowledge relating to biological resources (Elumalai, 2012).
6. Resolution 1803 (XVII) provides that States and international organizations shall strictly and conscientiously respect the sovereignty of peoples and nations over their natural wealth and resources in accordance with the Charter of the United Nations and the principles contained in the resolution. http://legal.un.org/avl/ha/ga_1803/ga_1803.html. Accessed on March 26, 2015.
7. According to a report prepared by the Director-General and adopted by the 21st Session of the Conference 'plant genetic resources should be considered as a common heritage of mankind and be available without restrictions for plant breeding, scientific and development purposes to all countries and institutions concerned' (http://www.fao.org/docrep/x5563E/X5563e0a.htm. Accessed on March 30, 2015).
8. The term 'biodiversity hotspot' is coined by Norman Myers. The areas where natural ecosystems are largely intact, but a large number of species that are rarely found outside the hotspot are endemic are called biodiversity hotspots. So far 34 biodiversity hotspots all over the world have been identified.

9. Among the plant-rich countries of the World, India ranks 10th, and in the context of Asian countries, her position is fourth.
10. This plant, a small rhizomatous, perennial herb, is available in India, Malaysia and Sri Lanka. The sub-species found in India is called *trichopuszeylanicus-travancoricus*. It grows at an altitude of around 1,000 meters in southern part of India, mainly in Western Ghats belongs to Tirunelveli district of Tamil Nadu and Thrivananthapuram district of Kerala (Gupta, WIPO).
11. Customary law is a set of customs, practices and beliefs that are accepted as obligatory rules of conduct by indigenous peoples and local communities. Customary law forms an intrinsic part of their social and economic systems and way of life (WIPO, Background brief 7). Such laws can serve as the fundamental legal basis or source of law for a community's legal rights over traditional knowledge and a factual element in establishing a community's collective rights over traditional knowledge.
12. Traditional knowledge registries may be internal or external, as well as it may be private or public. If registries are established and maintained within a community, they are called internal. The registries which are established and maintained outside the community are called external. External registries are maintained outside the community, often on the national or international level, by governments, non-governmental

organizations, museums or libraries. These registries can again be collections of TK specific to a particular community or to several communities (Hansen & Vanfleet, 2003).

However, more important is the distinction between private and public registries. Public registries place information in the public domain, but private registries do not. Since the information in a private registry is documented but is not in the public domain, it may not constitute prior art capable of preventing a patent based on the knowledge by an outsider. The knowledge in a private registry cannot prevent the approval of a patent under most IP systems unless it is considered prior art through a *sui generis* mechanism and disclosed to patent authorities (Hansen & Vanfleet, 2003). Private registries can be useful only if patent offices are made aware of the existence of such a registry. However, it may be possible to challenge and revoke a patent with knowledge documented in a private registry if patent law recognizes prior art not disclosed to public as is being admissible under a *sui generis* system.

13. Up to 2011 India managed to sign such an agreement with the European patent office and patent offices of Australia, Canada, Germany, the United Kingdom and the United States.

14. This information is available at http://www.ulwazi.org/index.php5?title=Main_Page.

15. 'Biological resources' means plants, animals and micro-organisms or parts thereof, their genetic material and

byproducts (excluding value added products) with actual or potential use or value, but does not include human genetic material (Section 2 (c)).

16. 'Benefit claimers' means the conservers of biological resources, their byproducts, creators and holders of knowledge and information relating to the use of such biological resources, innovations and practices associated with such use and application (Section 2 (a)).

17. The State shall designate or establish a National Competent Authority which shall implement and enforce the provisions of this legislation (Part 7.57 of African Model Law).

18. The Model Law Provisions 1982, Panama Special Intellectual Regime Law 2000 and South-Pacific Model Law 2002 make provision for indefinite period of protection.

19. The Section 18. (1) of GI Act,1999 reads as 'the registration of a geographical indication shall be for a period of 10 years, but may be renewed from time to time in accordance with the provisions of this section'.

20. The Section 18. (2) of GI Act,1999 reads as 'the registration of an authorised user shall be for a period of 10 years or for the period till the date on which the registration of the geographical indication in respect of which the authorised user is registered expires, whichever is earlier'.

21. However, there may be exceptions to this. The knowledge regarding the use of 'triphala', for instance, is well-known to almost all parts of our country. This herbal product is used for ailments of stomach. Since raw materials of 'triphala' are available in a defined geographical area, it is eligible for getting protection under the Geographical Indication Act. A geographical indication can be obtained if at least one of the activities of either the production or processing or preparation of the goods concerned takes place in the defined territory (Chavan, 2013).

REFERENCES

Abhilash, B. (2012). Legal protection of traditional medicine in the Neo-capitalist world – A legal analysis. Thesis, University of Kerala.

Balasubramaniam, K. (1987, May). Pharmaceutical patents in developing countries: Policy options. *Economic and Political Weekly*, 22, 19–21.

Baxter, B., Mayer, S., & Wijeratna, A. (1999). Crops and robbers: Biopiracy and the patenting of staple food crops. A Preliminary Findings of an Action Aid Investigation. Action Aid: London. Retrieved from http://www.actionaid.org

Bhattacharya, S. (2014). Bioprospecting, biopiracy and food security in India: The emerging sides of neoliberalism. *International Letters of Social and Humanistic Sciences*, *23*.

Bhukta, A. (2017). Role of traditional knowledge digital library in protecting India's traditional knowledge. In D. Bhowmik (Ed.), *Developmental issues of tribes*. New Delhi: Shandilya Publications.

Boisvert, V., & Vivien, F.-D. (2005). The convention on biological diversity: A conventionalist approach. *Ecological Economics*, *53*. Retrieved from www.elsevier.com/locate/ecolecon

Brahmi, P., Dua, R. P., & Dhillon, B. S. (2004). The Biological Diversity Act of India and agro-biodiversity management. *Current Science*, *86*(5).

Brown, P. (2002). Lack of cash puts gene banks in jeopardy. *The Guardian*, August 30.

Brundtland, G. (1987). Report of the World Commission on Environment and Development: Our common future. United Nations General Assembly document A/42/427

CBD. (1992). About 8(j), Introduction. Retrieved from https://www.cbd.int/traditional/intro.shtml. Accessed on April 1, 2015.

Chapman, K. (2009). *The final chapter in the "Enola" case has closed*. Retrieved from https://casipblog.wordpress.com/2009/09/17. Accessed on September 1, 2018.

Chavan, R. S. (2013). Legal protection of geographical indications: National and international perspective. Thesis, Karnataka University, Dharwad.

CIPR. (2002). *Integrating intellectual property rights and development policy report of the commission on intellectual property rights*. London: Commission on Intellectual Property Rights.

Cottier, T., & Panizzon, M. (2004, June). Legal perspectives on traditional knowledge: The case for intellectual property protection. *Journal of International Economic Law*, *7*(2), 371–399.

Cullet, P. (2005). Intellectual property protection and sustainable development. *Economic and Political Weekly*, *40*(32).

Damodaran, A. (2008). Traditional knowledge, intellectual property rights and biodiversity conservation: Critical issues and key challenges. *Journal of Intellectual Property Rights*, *13*.

Das, P. K. (2011). Legal protection of the traditional knowledge and traditional cultural expression in India: An appraisal. a thesis submitted to Burdwan University, West Bengal.

Das, A. (2015). An Analytical Study of Indian Copy Right Act, 1957 and Copyright Bill 2012. *International Journal of Innovative Research in Science, Engineering and Technology*, *4*(7).

Deccan Chronicle. (2017). Shashi Tharoor to Move Bill on Traditional Knowledge; Mar 9, 2017.

Deeva. (2002). Protection of traditional knowledge under new patent regime: Emerging issues. Thesis, Aligarh Muslim University, Aligarh.

Dhar, B., & Rao, N. (1992). Dunkel draft on TRIPS: Complete denial of developing countries interests. *Economic and Political Weekly*, *27*(6).

Dobkin de Rios, M., & Rumrrill, R. (2008). *Globalization and the future of ayahuasca: A Hallucinogenic tea, laced with controversy*. Westport, CT: Praeger Publishers.

Down to Earth. (2002). *Rooting out biopiracy*, November 15.

Downes, G. (2003). Implications of trips for food security in the majority world. Retrieved from www.comhlamh.org

Dureja, C. (2015). Historical development of copyright law in India. *International Journal of Advanced Research in Management and Social Sciences*, *4*(1). Retrieved from www.garph.co.uk

Dutfield, G. (1999). Protecting and revitalising traditional ecological knowledge: Intellectual property rights and community knowledge databases in India. In M. Blakeney (Ed.), *Intellectual property aspects of Ethno-biology*. London: Sweet and Maxwell.

Elumalai, S. (2012). International law on intellectual property rights and traditional knowledge: Evolving jurisprudence. Thesis, Tamilnadu Dr. Ambedkar Law University, Chennai.

ETC Group. (2002). DuPont and monsanto – Living in synergy? Retrieved from http://www.etcgroup.org/article.asp?newsid=315

EXIM Bank. (1997). Study on export potential of ayurveda and siddha products and services.

FAO. Trade in medicinal plants. Rome: A FAO Publication. Retrieved from http://www.fao.org/3/af285e/af285e00.pdf

FAO. (2009). *A global treaty for food security and sustainable agriculture*. International treaty on plant genetic resources for food and agriculture. Rome: A FAO Publication.

Fecteau, L. M. (2001). The ayahuasca patent revocation: Raising questions about current U.S. Patent policy. *Boston College Third World Law Journal, 21*.

Ghose, J. R. (2004). *Benefit sharing of genetic resources: The convention on biodiversity, the Bonn guidelines and emerging ABS framework*. Briefing Paper I, Gene Campaign, New Delhi.

Grain. (2001). Intellectual property rights: Ultimate control of agricultural R and D in Asia. Retrieved from www.grain.org/publications/asiaipr-en.cfm. Accessed on July 10, 2018.

Greiber, T., Moreno, S. P., Åhrén, M., Carrasco, J. N., Kamau, E. C., Medaglia, J. C., … Williams, C. (2012). *An explanatory guide to the nagoya protocol on access and benefit-sharing*. Gland: IUCN.

Hammond, E. (2015). Amid controversy and irony, Costa Rica's INBio surrenders biodiversity collections and lands to the State. Retrieved from www.twn.my/title2/biotk/2015/btk150401.htm. Accessed on August 31, 2018.

Hansen, S. A., & VanFleet, J. W. (2003). Traditional knowledge and intellectual property right: A handbook on issues and options foe traditional knowledge holders in protecting their intellectual property and maintaining and biological diversity. *American Association for the Advancement of Science (AAAS)*, Retrieved from http://Shr.Aaas.Org/Tek/Handbook

Hirwade, M., & Hirwade, A. (2012). Traditional knowledge protection: An Indian prospective. *DESIDOC Journal of Library & Information Technology*, *32*(3).

INBio. (1991). *Summary of terms-collaboration agreement: INBio-merck & Co., inc.* San Jose, Costa Rica: Instituto Nacional de Biodiversidad.

Kuriakose, T. (2010). Legal analysis of international policy response to the protection of traditional knowledge. Thesis, Jawaharlal Neheru University, New Delhi.

Laird, S., & Wynberg, R. (2008). *Access and benefit-sharing in practice: Trends in partnerships across sectors.* CBD technical series No. 38. Montreal, QC: The Secretariat of the Convention on Biological Diversity.

Long, D. E. (2012). Trade secrets and traditional knowledge: Strengthening international protection of indigenous innovation. Retrieved from http://ssrn.com/abstract=2214785

Lukose L. P. (2009). Protection of traditional knowledge as intellectual property – with special reference to India. Thesis, Mahatma Gandhi University, Kottayam.

Meek, J. (2000). Beginners guide to gene patents. *The Guardian*, November 15. Retrieved from https://www.theguardian.com/science/2000/nov/15/genetics.theissuesexplained

Merck & Co, Inc. (1993). *Searching for medicines while preserving the rainforest: The INBio-Merck agreement.* unpublished manuscript.

Mgbeoji, I. (2001). Patents and traditional knowledge of the uses of plants: Is a communal patent regime part of the solution to the scourge of bio piracy. *Indiana Journal of Global Legal Studies*, *9*(1), Article 9. Retrieved from http://www.repository.law.indiana.edu/ijgls/vol9/iss1/9

Muller, M. R. (2004). An analysis of the implications of intellectual property rights (IPR) on the Global Biodiversity Information Facility (GBIF). Retrieved from http://dlc.dlib.indiana.edu/dlc/bitstream/handle/10535/3831/ipr_final.pdf

Muro, P. De., & Mazziotta, M. (2010). Towards a food insecurity multidimensional index. Retrieved from nitropdf.com/professional. Accessed on July 8, 2018.

Nair, M. D. (2011). TRIPS, WTO and IPR: Protection of bioresources and traditional knowledge. *Journal of Intellectual Property Rights*, *16*.

Naresh, (2012). Intellectual property rights with special reference to biodiversity management and sustainable development. Thesis, Maharshi Dayanand University, Rohtak.

Nayar, D. (1992). Intellectual property rights and LDCs : Some strategic issues. *Economic and Political Weekly*, *27*(6).

New agriculturist. (2009). Retrieved from http://www.new-ag.info/en/developments/devItem.php?a=964

Nghihalwa, S. L. (2014). An analysis of the registration of traditional product names, terms, symbols and other cultural expressions as trademarks in Namibia. Thesis, University of Cape Town, Rondebosch.

NISCAIR. (2003). Annual report, 2002-03.

Nordell, P. J. (1957). The notion of originality – Redundant or not? Retrieved from http://www.scandinavianlaw.se/pdf/42-7.pdf. Accessed on April22, 2018.

Nunez, R. G. (2007). Intellectual property and the protection of traditional knowledge, genetic resources and folklore: The Peruvian experience, *Max Planck Yearbook of United Nations Law*, *12*, 487–549.

Ogwezzy, M. C. (2012). Indigenous or traditional knowledge under intellectual property laws: An examination of the efficacy of copyright law, trade secret and sui generis rights. *International and Comparative Law Review*, *12*(1), 7–37. doi: 10.1515/iclr-2016-0076

Pant, R. (2015). *Protecting and promoting traditional knowledge in India: What role for geographical indications?* IIED working paper. IIED, London. Retrieved from http://pubs.iied.org/16576IIED

Pant, A., & Moorthy, A. L. (2013). Knowledge management and safeguarding Indian traditional knowledge. *Annals of Library and Information Studies*, *60*.

Patro, L. (2016). Medicinal plants of India: With special reference to odisha. *IJARIIE*, *2*(5).

Poorna, R. L., Mymoon, M., & Hariharan, A. (2014). Preservation and protection of traditional knowledge - diverse documentation initiatives across the globe. *Current Science*, *107*(8).

Pryor, G. (1991). The case for defensive disclosure. *Software Patent Institute*, Retrieved from http://www.spi.org/defdis.htm

Pushpangadan P., Rajasekharan, S., Ratheshkumar, P. K., Jawahar, C. R., Velayudhan Nair, V., Lakshmi, N., & Sarada Amma, L. (1988). 'Arogyappacha' (Trichopus Zeylanicus

Gaertn), the 'Ginseng' of Kani tribes of Agasthyar hills (Kerala) for evergreen health and vitality. *Ancient Science of Life*, *VIII*(1).

Raju, K. D. (2004). WTO-TRIPS obligations and patent amendments in India: A critical stocktaking. *Journal of Intellectual Property Rights*, *9*.

Rangel, G. (2015). From Corgis to corn: A brief look at the long history of GMO technology. Retrieved from sitn.hms.harvard.edu/flash/2015. Accessed on April 10, 2017.

Robinson, D. F. (2010). *Patent-related biopiracy cases. Confronting biopiracy: Challenges, cases and international debates*. London; Washington, DC: Earthscan.

Sahai, S. (2004). Commercialization of traditional knowledge and benefit. In S. Twarog, & P. Kapoor (Eds.), *Protecting and promoting traditional knowledge: Systems, national experiences and international dimensions*. (pp. 279–292) Geneva: UNCTAD.

Seth, Y. (2017). Government looks to bring out seeds bill from cold storage, push for passage. *The Economic Times*, ET Bureau, updated: Feb 14, 2017. Retrieved from https://economictimes.indiatimes.com/news/politics-and-nation/government-looks-to-bring-out-seeds-bill-from-cold-storage-push-for-passage/articleshow/57135472.cms?from=mdr

Sharma, D. (2002). Digital library on Indian medicine systems: Another tool for biopiracy. *Economic and Political Weekly*, *37*.

Shirolikar, M. (2011). History and evolution of trademark system. Retrieved from www.bananaip.com. Accessed on April 30, 2018.

Shiva, V. (1993). *Monocultures of the mind: Perspectives on biodiversity and biotechnology*. London and New Jersey: Zed Books.

Singh, S. P. (2015). The seeds bill 2011: Seeking to promote use of quality seeds by regulating production, distribution, sale, export and import. Retrieved from www.parfore.in/BillBlowups.htm

Suh, J., & MacPherson, A. (2007). The impact of geographical indication on the revitalisation of a regional economy: A case study of 'boseong' green tea. *Area, 39*(4).

Swamy, R. N. (2014). Protection of traditional knowledge in the present IPR regime: A mirage or a reality. *Indian Journal of Public Administration, LX*(1).

Torsen, M., & Anderson, J. (2010). *Intellectual property and the safeguarding of traditional cultures: Legal issues and practical options for museums, libraries and archives*. Geneva: An WIPO Publication.

Tully, S. (2003). The Bonn guidelines on access togenetic resources and benefit sharing. *RECIEL, 12*(1).

Tupper, K. W. (2009). Ayahuasca healing beyond the Amazon: The globalization of a traditional indigenous entheogenic practice. *Global Networks, 9*

UNDP. (2001). *Human development report*. UNDP, New York, NY.

UNDP. (2003). *Making global trade work for people*, New York, NY: UNDP.

UNEP. (2002). *Bonn guidelines on access to genetic resources and fair and equitable sharing of the benefits arising out of their Utilization*.

Varadarajan, D. (2011). A trade secret approach to protecting traditional knowledge. *Yale Journal of International Law, 36*.

Varkay, E. (2007). Traditional knowledge – The changing scenario in India. Retrieved from www.law.ed.ac.uk/ahrb/publications/online/varkey.htm

Venkataraman, K., & Latha, S. S. (2008). Intellectual property rights, traditional knowledge and biodiversity of India. *Journal of Intellectual Property Rights, 13*.

Vivas-Eugui, D., Ruiz, M., & Espinosa, M. F. (2003). *International processes on genetic resources and traditional knowledge: Options and negotiation alternatives*. An informal background paper. Retrieved from http://www.planttreaty.org/content/international-processes-genetic-resources-and-traditional-knowledge-options-and-negotiation-. Accessed on March 22, 2015

Wekundah, J. M. (2012). *Why protect traditional knowledge?* Special Series, No.44. African technology Policy Studies Network, Biotechnology Trust Africa.

WHO. (1991). *Guidelines for the assessment of herbal medicine, Program on Traditional Medicine*. Geneva: World Health Organization.

WHO. (2012). Promoting access to medical technologies and innovation: Intersections between public Health, Intellectual Property and Trade. Retrieved from https://www.wto.org/english/res_e/booksp_e/pamtiwhowipowtoweb13_e.pdf

WIPO. (2002). Traditional Knowledge – Operational Terms and Definitions; WIPO/GRTKF/IC/3/9; Intergovernmental Committee on Intellectual Property and Genetic Resources, Traditional Knowledge and Folklore, WIPO.

WIPO. (2003). *Consolidated analysis of the legal protection of traditional cultural expressions/expressions of folklore.* Background Paper 1. Retrieved from https://www.wipo.int/publications/en/details.jsp?id=285

WIPO. (2012, July 9–13). Glossary of key terms related to intellectual property and genetic resources, traditional knowledge and traditional cultural expressions. Twenty-Second Session, Geneva. Retrieved from https://www.wipo.int/meetings/en/doc_details.jsp?doc_id=410022

WIPO. (2017). *Geographical indications: An introduction.* Geneva: An WIPO Publication.

Wynberg, R. (2004). Rhetoric, realism and benefit sharing: Use of traditional knowledge of *Hoodia* species in the development of an appetite suppressant. *Journal of World Intellectual Property*, 7(6), 851–876.

Wynberg, R. (2010). Hot air over hoodia. *Seedling*, October.

INDEX

www.ingramcontent.com/pod-product-compliance
Lightning Source LLC
LaVergne TN
LVHW022215200926
848481LV00006B/1982
9781800430662